Two Tickets and a Feather

PRESENT ALASKA—FUTURE OF HER PAST
ANOTHER ALASKAN MYSTERY

by Marianne Schlegelmilch

Publication Consultants
Since 1978

PO Box 221974 Anchorage, Alaska 99522-1974
books@publicationconsultants.com—www.publicationconsultants.com

I0132411

ISBN 978-1-59433-221-0
eBook 978-1-59433-222-7
Library of Congress Catalog Card Number: 2011925136

Cover Art by Barb Montpas Sirmeyer

Copyright 2010 Marianne Schlegelmilch
—First Edition—

Manufactured in the United States of America.

Dedication

To Janet

Mara Speaks

Here, standing on this deck for the last time at this place where I have worked for nearly the past year—this square, yellow, two-story building that personifies old-town Homer for me—I find myself reflecting on everything that got me here.

Could it have been anything other than destiny that led me to this place? That brought me to this job with Ocean Research and Preserve, this place staffed with a crew of wonderful people—strangers to me at first, but now friends—this place that has provided the only real focus in my life during the unbelievable turmoil that marked my arrival in Alaska?

The way the waves are pounding right now—they're the same sound I have listened to every day I have come to work. Their rhythmic crash onto Bishop's Beach across the street soothes me. Who of us wouldn't be lulled into glorious peace by this sound? It was right from that beach that I took my first samples for my research on sea plankton. It is that beach I look down at from my home farther up the bluff. I'm going to miss this place and this work, but mostly, I'm going to miss the friends I have made here.

It's not that life is taking a downward turn. After everything that's gone on in the last year, where else is there to go but up? All of this—Alaska, this job, living here—all of this was supposed to have been a new chapter in my life after losing Brad. How could I ever have guessed that he would turn up alive, right here in Alaska, after having been missing and presumed dead for more years than we had even known each other in college and our marriage combined? Could anybody ever have imagined my complete shock at finding him right in the place I was visiting, only to see him gunned down dead before my eyes? I can't even believe now that this is my life I am remembering. It sounds like something out of a mystery novel or some action/adventure movie.

Well, I'm not going to stand here all day in this wind thinking about the past. I've already thought about it too much. After all, isn't it enough that I lived it? I have to let it go—stop thinking about it. I need to focus on looking at all this beauty around me. This is my world now—my life. Doug was right to bring us here. He needed this as much as I did after seeing his own brother murdered. Weird, how something so awful as two murders could bring us together like they did—Doug losing Dan right before I lost Brad.

I guess on some level I knew we would end up married when Thor found the ring I accidentally dropped overboard from the ferry on the way up to Alaska. That reminds me, I need to pick up some dog food for Thor on the way home. And Doug said he needed to do some work on the seiner this afternoon, so I'd better think of something for dinner that I can take down to him at the harbor.

Yes, time's a-wasting if I'm going to get on with this day. I can't stand here looking at the bay and the mountains for the rest of my life, thinking of what was. No, I have things to do and I can't think about the past anymore when my present and future seem so right.

Well, I could, but I'm going to do it from our seiner, just as soon as we head out to sea next week. It's going to be quite the adventure.

Chapter One

Joe Michael's Gift

Stepping down from the deck of the building that housed Ocean Research and Preserve, Mara looked at the whitecaps on the deep blue waters of the Inlet as the waves thundered on the beach below the bluff on which she stood. A few seiners, recognizable by their distinctive design, bobbed in the choppy seas. She closed her eyes tightly as if to seal in the sight. It should always be this way—always and forever it should remain this same quaint little town.

The way the snowy mountains across the Inlet glowed against the deep blue sky made today seem more beautiful than ever, but tomorrow she expected she would say the same thing, just as she would the next day, and the next day, and the next. It's just the way it was for almost everyone she knew here in Homer, Alaska—just another day in Paradise—like the locals said.

Opening the envelope that she had just been given in the office, she was surprised to see a lifetime pass for the Alaska State ferry with her name, *Mara Williams,* written on it. Eagerly, she read the short attached note.

Dear Woman-who-trips-on-the-ferry,

I meant to give this to you in person, but as you can see, it didn't work out. My people will get it to you, though, so I know you will have it if you need it.

The ferry is your link to your freedom.

This pass is your means to be free.

Keep this freedom between you and me.

Joe Michael

When she went back inside to try to find out who had delivered the note, as far as anyone knew, it had simply turned up in the mailbox yesterday— hand-delivered and addressed simply, *to Mara Williams.*

Once back outside, she placed the note and the ticket carefully inside her pocket, climbed into Doug's old beater truck, slammed the door three times before it would latch, turned the ignition an equal number of times before the engine would start, and drove off. When she got to the harbor, she could see Doug standing on the deck of the seiner, which was floating in water about 15 feet below the parking area due to the low tide.

"Your SUV's ready over at the repair shop," he called up to her. "I would have picked it up for you, but I got hung up with this fouled fuel pump I've been working on here, and I'm gonna need to take a run into town to pick up a new one or we're not going anywhere anytime soon."

"I'm sorry I took so long," she told him. "Maybe you can drop me off on your way in and I'll drive myself back home and fix something to bring out to the seiner for us for dinner. I also have to stop at the store and get some more dog food."

She waited while he grabbed a rag and wiped the grease from his hands before locking his tools inside the cabin and climbing up to the docks. Moments later she moved over so he could slide into the driver's seat beside her, happy when he leaned over and kissed her just as he always did—as naturally as if he were breathing.

"Did everything go okay with turning in your resignation?" he asked her, putting the truck in reverse and backing slowly out of the space where she had parked behind one of the tourist-oriented shops-on-pilings that stood alongside the harbor.

"It did," she answered. "They said they really appreciated me being here for the past eleven months, and—"laughing"—they pretty much knew that I'd be leaving after taking all of last summer off to be with you out on the boat."

"That's good," Doug answered, making a right turn onto the Spit road and heading the 4 miles into town as she continued talking.

"They told me I could come back any time. They said good biologists are hard to find—especially those specializing in sea plankton, like me—Oh, Doug! Stop! Look—the otters!"

"Looks like a storm's coming in," Doug said matter-of-factly, while she snapped a few pictures of the rafts of sea otters in Mud Bay. Like most everyone in town, she knew the otters rafted up in this shallow area at the start of the Spit right before a storm, so she took advantage of the photo op using the camera she always carried.

When they reached the auto shop a few minutes later, she waited while Doug talked to the mechanic, checked the repairs, and made sure her SUV was running okay. Meanwhile, she went in to pay the bill and then switched vehicles with him, waiting while he walked to his truck. He pulled up alongside her on his way out of the parking lot, leaning with one elbow out the window as he spoke.

"Looks like you're about to change careers and become a fisherman," he teased.

The smile she flashed him was instant, making her stop fiddling for a moment with putting their checkbook back inside her purse. Fingering the note from Joe Michael in her pocket, she stuck it inside her bag along with their checkbook. She started to mention the note to Doug, but stopped herself before any words could come out. Instead, she blew him a kiss and drove off.

Marriage to Doug had brought more happiness than she could ever have hoped for so far, but they had been married only about a year. Her marriage to Brad had taught her that *perfect* could be an illusion. She would show the note to Doug when the time was right. For now, though, she didn't want to make him worry about a mysterious message from a man whose memorial service they had attended over a year ago.

CHAPTER TWO

Unsettling News

LATER, AFTER DISCOVERING THAT SHE HAD LOCKED HER KEYS IN HER SUV, Doug and Mara decided to spend the night on their boat. With night coming on, a gale setting in, and Doug's truck clear around the other side of the harbor, they had enjoyed the meal of hot soup and sandwiches that Mara had brought from home, and had gone to bed early. Despite the howling wind that clanged everything that was not secured tightly, Mara slept snuggly alongside Doug as the seiner tossed in the choppy waters of the Homer harbor. Curled up into a comfy ball on the floor beside them, slept their dog, Thor.

They were tired, having spent the better part of the afternoon getting ready to head out to sea tomorrow on the first fishing trip of the season. Mara had run errands in town while Doug had worked on replacing a fouled fuel pump and checking out the engine of the *Fire Ring Roamer* for any other problems.

He had been thorough, testing the fuel in both tanks to be sure there was no water that could cause another fuel pump problem, and he had double-checked filters, tightened caps and generally inspected the engine to make sure they would be ready to leave in the morning. Just in case, though, he had purchased a spare fuel pump to carry on board, since he had just replaced the current one six months earlier and already it had malfunctioned.

By the time morning came, the wind had died down so they walked to Doug's truck. Thor jump into the truck bed after Doug removed some odds and ends they wouldn't need and left them in storage, and they drove home to get Mara's extra set of keys so they could come back and pick up her SUV. Doug was the first to reach the phone that had been ringing since they walked in.

"Hi Sarah. Yeah, we slept on the boat last night because Mara locked her keys in the car. What do you mean, news? What kind of news? Everything's okay with you and the baby, isn't it? You're not in early labor or anything? We don't want that baby born a whole three months early, now . . ."

By now Mara was standing with her face alongside her husband's, straining to hear the conversation while he held the phone slightly away from his ear. Having her best friend finally living here in Alaska made her smile almost as much as did hearing her patiently answer, one by one, all the questions that Doug was bombarding her with.

Suddenly Doug's body tightened and he pulled the phone closer to his ear. It was obvious that the conversation had taken an alarming turn. Mara pulled on Doug's arm, silently urging him to move the phone away from his ear again as she strained to listen.

"Sassy's what?" Doug said. "Murdered? When?" Abruptly, he handed the phone to Mara. His face had gone pale and bore a look of shock.

Mara watched him as she took the phone. Doug's old girlfriend, Sassy? Dead? She prodded Sarah for details. Had Ken told her everything? After all, hadn't she said her husband had been the first police officer on the scene?

"Uh, huh. It's unbelievable, Sarah. Ken must have been so shocked to find it was Sassy. I know. Really? She was only thirty-seven? I know. I thought she was a lot younger, too. Everyone did. Does Ellie know yet? Okay, tell Ellie we send our love to her and Anna and we'll see them…probably tomorrow. Don't worry. Doug will be okay. It's just the shock, you know. Talk soon. Bye."

Placing the phone back in the receiver, she looked at Doug.

"I don't know what to say. I can't believe this is happening. Doug…I'm sorry. I know Sassy once meant so much to you."

"I thought all of this was behind us," Doug said, pacing nervously and scratching his head. "I know Sassy's done some horrible things, but I don't think she deserved this."

"Sarah said it was a gunshot that came right through Sassy's bedroom window while she slept," Mara told him. "They found shattered glass on the floor and the bullet wound in her head. Ken said that the IPA—they've already been called in—told him it was typical of a hit by one of the drug cartels. They found some other evidence to support that, I guess. Ken thinks Sassy probably never saw it coming."

"A.C. was never anything but trouble to his sister," Doug said, angrily. "Once I started hearing the rumors that he had gotten tied up with the drug cartels, I knew it was only a matter of time before someone offed him. I just wish it didn't have to be her that did it, but she saved your life—and probably Ellie's, too—and now it's cost her her own."

Mara ignored the sting of Doug's words.

"Ken told Sarah that the IPA thinks this is somehow tied in with Sassy shooting her brother and some drug lord thinking she knew more about

A.C.'s activities than she did. He said that members of the IPA, including Karen Steele, would be meeting with him in his office as soon as they fly in from Oregon—possibly as early as this afternoon."

Doug was becoming increasingly upset. "Sassy's a lot of things, but she was no drug runner."

"I know that," Mara said.

"Somehow I knew A.C. would bring her down, even if it was long after his own sorry ass was gone," Doug said. "I warned her all the time about having her bedroom on the first floor. Why didn't she listen to me? If she had, maybe…"

"I know you loved her once, and I know she killed Adam to save me," Mara said.

"I'm sorry," Doug said, pulling Mara close. "I don't mean to take this out on you. Of course I know you know all this. I mean, it was all almost predictable—you know—that it would turn out like this.

"Ever since they were kids Sassy's watched out for Adam. She never seemed to see his dark side as much as everyone else did—well, I shouldn't say that. I think she knew he was getting into too much trouble, but she always told me she thought he would straighten out one day. She wanted to believe that. After her own horrible life, in any way she could, she wanted to make a different world for A.C."

"No one would have wanted this for Sassy," Mara told her husband. "Not me, not Ellie, not even the people who judged her without ever knowing her."

For the next few minutes, neither of them said anything, until Mara spoke first.

"Sassy's not in pain anymore, Doug. And I believe she felt a certain peace after coming to terms with her own attempted suicide. She was trying to right all the wrongs. I believe she came to realize that we all knew that, and I'm glad we had enough time to help her forgive herself. After all, as much as she hurt others, in reality, it was herself she was hurting the most."

Doug nodded in somber agreement as Mara continued to fill him in on the details she had just obtained from Sarah.

"Sarah said there's not going to be a funeral. Also, Ken's going to boost security at Ellie's place for now. You know how often he's told us that he hasn't felt good about Ellie and Anna being there alone since Dan's murder last March."

Doug nodded, reassured that the trooper who had done so much to help solve his brother's murder was on top of things once again and would do all he could to protect Sarah's sister.

"I'll give Ellie a call and make sure she knows to call me if she needs me," Doug said. "I think we'd better take Thor up there to stay with them. I'd feel better knowing he's there."

Mara had to agree. They had already talked about leaving Thor up at Ellie's and leaving Anna in charge of feeding him. The seiner was too confining for a wolf-dog like Thor and, now that Anna was six, she was more than able to help her mother feed and care for him.

Thor knew the homestead, too, and he would be more comfortable there than out to sea for the next several months. They would visit him often once they were back—especially since Ellie was keeping Doug's old place in the bunkhouse ready for them.

"I was hoping Ken could retire from the police force next month without anymore hassles like this," Doug said. "Especially with the baby on the way. Looks like we're not done yet, although I can't imagine what else could happen."

"I can't imagine that there could be any more to this story, either—you know—especially now that the drug runners have gotten their revenge on Sassy for A.C.'s death. At least I hope not."

Mara hugged Doug as they stood holding each other for a moment. She still couldn't believe how much she loved him and how much he loved her. Fate had such a strange way of making things right.

"I'm sorry things had to go this way for Sassy, Doug. After all she'd been through, I had really hoped she would be okay now."

Chapter Three

In Search of Herring

Two days later, Doug and Mara left for Sitka and for the first herring fishery of the year after delaying their departure by one day to drive Thor up to stay with Ellie and Anna in Palmer. It was important to be in Sitka Sound when the herring moved in, which was usually in the last two weeks of March. Getting the prized roe before the herring spawned was key.

Doug had hired the same two deckhands he had worked with last year, and had bought them plane fare to Sitka, where they would be waiting when he arrived with the *Fire Ring Roamer*. He had already been coaching Mara on all the intricacies of the most fast-paced and highly competitive fishery in Alaska. Like many others, he hoped to make most of his year's earnings during the run, which this year was predicted to be one of the strongest on record.

He had also leased one of Ellie's planes, and Ellie was sending a pilot named Ben Donaley to be his fish spotter; a man she described as late middle-aged with an impressive resume. When learning of Doug's need for a spotter pilot, Ben had been the first to volunteer.

"Ben's been flying for me since right after you and Mara took off for Homer and got married," Ellie had told Doug. "I can't say enough good things about him. He's been a godsend since Dan died."

Doug had long held the belief that a good spotter pilot was essential in this particular fishery because the fishery was so short and the stakes were so high. As expensive as it would be, he wanted his own personal spotter rather than splitting the cost with several other boats.

Reports that Ben Donaley was already in Sitka becoming familiar with all the intricacies of working the fishery was welcome news. If Ellie said Ben was the best, then that was good enough for him, and Ellie had given him a good rate—one they both could live with and felt was fair to them both. If all went as planned, he and Mara would meet Ben Donaley in Sitka in about two days.

Doug's seiner would be among the fifty seiners participating this year. Two years ago he had made enough to pay off his boat. If this year was equally or more successful, it would mean he might be able to pay off the remaining loan on his permit, making the two-week investment in his time well worth the stress that the short fishery would bring. The delay in having to fix the fuel pump might have cost him a day, but he had allowed plenty of time for him and Mara to get to Sitka in advance of the herring run, so there was no reason to worry.

When the fuel pump went out again halfway to Sitka, his stress level went up a bit. Two fuel pumps going out—one right after the other. Something seemed strange about that. He had been particularly diligent in regularly checking his filters for water and emptying any he found. There did seem to be more water in the fuel than usual this trip and he had wracked his brain to figure out why, even making sure that the gas cap was tight and no depression or dent had occurred around the opening that would cause water to accumulate during the oversplash in heavy seas.

This would be a good opportunity to teach Mara how to tear a fuel pump apart, and so he called her over and they laid out some rags and did just that.

Just as he suspected, there was water inside the pump, so he proceeded to change all the filters and check all the fittings for tightness, even though he had just done all that right before leaving two days ago. He took pains to go slowly so that Mara could learn, even encouraging her to do the work while he coached her. He was more than impressed when she handled the job just fine.

When they were done, he radioed a couple of nearby seiners that he knew had also just left from Homer, just to see if maybe the problem was fouled fuel. Since no one else had reported any similar trouble, he would ease his concerns by hiring a mechanic for a second opinion when they got to Sitka, just to make sure everything was okay.

There was a full rainbow over Sitka Sound when they arrived.

"This is just beautiful," Mara said, standing beside him on the deck. "Two perfect visits to Sitka—the first when I married you and the second as your first mate on the seiner."

Doug hugged her and had to agree. "Maybe Sitka is our destiny," he said.

After Doug tied up his seiner, he found a mechanic who would look at his engine tomorrow. He had checked and double checked everything on his boat before leaving and then again while at sea. The recurrence of water in the fuel was troublesome. Maybe the mechanic could track the problem down.

He and Mara checked into the Shee Atika Hotel next to the harbor. They could see the *Fire Ring Roamer* from the hotel restaurant as they ate breakfast the next morning and the morning after that. After hearing the full story of the problems Doug described, the mechanic had told him that he was going to take his time and go through everything on the boat. With the start of the herring fishery still several days away, Doug gave the mechanic the go-ahead. The seiner was overdue for a thorough independent inspection anyway, so might as well kill two birds with one stone and get some reassurance in the process.

"Strange," the mechanic told Doug two days later. "Both fuel tanks tested just fine—no obvious cracks or seals leaking, loose fittings or anything like that, but there was quite a bit of water in the tank when I tested it. I know you said you tested it just before leaving Homer."

"I put a stick down there the night before we left," Doug told him. "Everything seemed fine."

"It's possible that condensation could be the problem," the mechanic said. "The amount of water I found in your tank looks kind of suspicious, though, especially since you told me you just went through everything and had it all in top-notch shape, and that you checked both tanks for water before you left. Even though you hate to think of it happening, it kinda makes you wonder. I'd say either you got hold of some fouled fuel, or worse yet, someone's been dumpin' water in your fuel tank. There's just no other explanation I can come up with."

"Something weird's going on with the seiner," Doug told Mara later, as he explained what the mechanic had told him. "There was no water in the fuel tanks when I checked them after filling them Wednesday night, but they've got water now, and no one can figure out where it's coming from. As much as I don't like to think like this—and the mechanic is the one who first brought this up—it makes you wonder if someone tampered with the tanks. If so, it had to have happened sometime during the night or maybe Thursday when we took Thor up to Palmer. I should've kept the deckhands in town on the boat instead of sending them to Sitka last week, I guess."

"It could just be kids," Mara told him after being reminded that none of the other boats had had fuel problems. "I've heard other people say there's been a spate of vandalism on the Spit lately."

"Could be," Doug answered, dialing the phone to call the fuel supplier at the Homer harbor.

"The manager says he's sure the fuel is okay," Doug told her after hanging up. "He said they haven't had any other complaints and that they just had an inspector down for routine testing the same morning we filled up. He said that on a normal day he could give me a 98% assurance that it wasn't the fuel, but in this particular case, he could make that 100%. Fouled fuel's not the problem—that's what he told me."

Mara didn't know what to say. The thought that somebody might have been tampering with the seiner made her just as uneasy as it did Doug.

"I'm going to talk to the harbormaster about beefing up security in Homer harbor as soon as we get back," Doug told her. "Meanwhile, I'm going to keep my extra filters and supplies locked up and maybe even think about bringing Thor down for a while when we get home."

That night they had dinner with Ben Donaley. He was a tall, gray-haired man with a comfortable demeanor and a quick smile that sharply contrasted with the intensity in his eyes. Both Doug and Mara liked him instantly and before their dinner had even arrived, were deep in conversation about the fishery and how they would approach it. Mara sensed a certain familiarity about this man that she couldn't explain, but she was certain—well, almost certain—that she had never seen or met Ben Donaley before.

After dinner, she walked toward the elevator in the hotel while Doug stopped in the restroom. Why did she feel uneasy? Was she just imagining that Ben was watching her from the lobby? Maybe she was just being silly. Ignoring any discomfort she felt, she waved to him and smiled. He waved back just as Doug joined her and waved, too, before they got on the elevator to go up to their room. She told Doug about it later. "It wasn't anything creepy with the way he looked at me or anything like that—just kind of a wistful look. I feel silly even bringing it up to you now that I have."

"It's not just you, Mara," Doug told her. "I got that feeling myself as we talked through dinner. It was almost as if he thought he knew us, but knew he really didn't—if that makes any sense."

"Well, he seems like a really nice man and Ellie sure thinks the world of him," Mara answered.

Pausing to look at her feet for a moment, she continued, "There's something I've been meaning to show you and now that we are talking about strange vibes…"

Mara reached into her purse and handed the ferry ticket she had been given at work to Doug. "I got this along with a note from Joe at work the other day."

"Joe?" Doug said.

"Joe Michael," Mara answered, instantly reminding Doug of the recently deceased Native man whose gift of a feather had kept Mara safe from numerous brushes with danger since her arrival in Alaska.

"That's weird," Doug told her, taking a folded ferry ticket out of his pocket and handing it to her with its accompanying note. "I got this, too—right before we left Homer. One of the fishermen told me a Native guy handed it to him in the harbor and asked him to get it to me, saying to tell me that he was the one who told me about Joe's funeral last spring. I forgot to mention it to you in all the commotion of leaving and the fuel pump issues."

Mara read Doug's note after he read hers:

Makes no sense

In present tense

Just take heed

When you see the need

-J.M.~now R.I.P.

Two lifetime passes for the Alaska State ferry—one for each of them—each with a note signed by a man who they knew to be dead. Looking at each other, neither of them said anything as they walked into their room.

CHAPTER FOUR

Waiting

On the fourth day in Sitka, anxious for the first sign of herring, Doug met with Ben Donaley and his two crewmen over breakfast.

"Word is that someone spotted a mass of herring off Chichagof Island last night," Ben said, before excusing himself to go meet with a couple of other pilots. "I flew out this morning and there was no sign of 'em."

"I say let's keep her fueled up and ready to move on a moment's notice," Doug told his crew. "We'll stay in touch on the cell phone, huh, Ben?"

Ben nodded in agreement as he walked off, leaving Doug to finish breakfast with his two deckhands.

The youngest, Jason Kent, had been Doug's deckhand for the past two seasons, having worked with one of the Sitka-based fishermen last year, but only because Doug hadn't fished that season. He was a twenty-something young man with a good head on his shoulders and a loyalty that had impressed Doug right from the moment he had first hired him a couple of years ago.

The jitney operator, Paul Hanson, had been working with Doug on and off for 15 years and knew the *Fire Ring Roamer* almost as well as Doug did. He was in his forties and as experienced at sea as anyone. Doug knew that with Paul on his crew, he was working with one of the best.

"I don't wanna alarm ya, Doug," Paul said, taking Doug aside, "but I caught someone snoopin' around the seiner last night about ten. I heard somethin' clang out on the dock and looked out an' saw this guy jump back from the side of the boat."

"Sure it wasn't just a drunk or a tourist?" Doug asked him.

"Didn't look to be drunk," Hanson told him. "Got kinda spooked when I stuck my head out of the cabin and he just backed away into the dark. I hollered for 'im to keep his sorry ass outta paid dock space if he wanted to keep two cheeks to sit down on."

"Well, you get all kinds around here," Doug said. "Especially about that time of the night when they've all had a chance to stop across the street at the P bar and have a couple."

"Yeah…yer prob'ly right. Just thought I'd mention it, ya know…"

"I appreciate it, Paul," Doug replied. "And I appreciate knowing you've got my back."

What Doug didn't say was that he was more than a little concerned about what Hanson had just told him, especially in view of the issues with the fuel pump and fuel tank—and maybe even in view of the fact that Sassy had been murdered only days ago. Although they were now a good 700 miles or more from Homer and another 300 road miles from Palmer, after what he had seen happen with his brother, the murder of Mara's husband, and with Sassy and her brother in the last year, nothing at this point would surprise him. Maybe he was a little more antsy than he should be. Pushing thoughts of the fuel pump and Hanson's story out of his mind, he went up to the room to pick up Mara.

"I heard the ferry was going to be in at noon. It might be a good time to get our passes authenticated so we have them if and when we need them."

Mara furrowed her brow. "I think you're right, Doug. With everything that's happened with Joe Michael and the feather, we can't afford not to take this seriously."

With the tickets in hand, Doug led his wife down the stairs to the lobby. Even though Joe was now dead, somehow the old man had found it necessary to leave a vague warning for each of them—a warning that he would make sure both he and Mara listened to.

They stepped out the door just in time to catch the shuttle to the ferry terminal, which was some 4 or 5 miles down Halibut Point Road northwest of town.

CHAPTER FIVE

Present of the Past

Erin De la Corte unlocked the front door to her mother's house outside Palmer, Alaska and walked inside. Immediately, she was taken aback by the humble surroundings of the small, one-story ranch that sat on 15 acres of flat land, surrounded by some of the most majestic mountains she had ever seen. In the distance, she could hear the roar of racing cars, and she could smell their exhaust in the cool clear air of the sunny Sunday afternoon.

A pair of boots caked in dried mud sat beside the door. A rumpled canvas jacket hung on a hook in the entry. Right beside it hung a well-worn wide-brimmed felt hat, and hanging from a hook next to the coat rack was a red horse's bridle and other assorted tack. On the floor directly below, a dusty striped saddle blanket lay in a heap.

Erin hung her own coat on the last available hook and walked into the living room. Through the sheer white curtains that hung over the windows, she could see several horses in a field just beyond the house. A woodstove in the corner still felt warm to the touch, even though nothing but ashes remained inside the box. A vole scurried across the floor and out a crack near the bottom of a door that stood on the back wall at about the invisible place where the living room ended and the dining area began.

A flashing red light blinked on the answering machine that sat on the long counter that separated the dining area from the kitchen. Erin reached out toward the message button, hesitated for a moment and then pushed it, sitting on a stool near the counter to listen to the four messages it held.

One by one she listened—each message a snippet of her mother's life punctuated by the beeps that separated them. She was struck by the normalcy of them. For a moment, she wished she could have known this woman who was her birth mother. Her real mother, the one who had raised her since infancy, was much different. Erin had come here with her blessing, after learning of the shooting.

Erin knew that Monica De la Corte had always held Amanda Carlson in high regard. Monica had often told her adoptive daughter that as far as she was concerned, any girl of fifteen who could choose to let the innocent, unborn product of rape have a chance at life, and who would even bequeath the child her own deceased mother's name, deserved all the support that a woman of privilege like herself could impart. It was in that spirit that she had provided Amanda Carlson with regular updates on her daughter's childhood, including pictures and drawings Erin had brought home from the private school she attended near Santa Barbara.

Erin opened the top drawer of the dining room hutch and lifted those pictures from under the table linens where she had found them earlier when rummaging through the room. Until now, she hadn't been aware of this closeness between the woman she called her mother and the woman who had given her life. She thumbed through the precious childhood mementos, remembering each one as she did. Here in the house where her real mother had lived, she gave thanks that she had been able to meet her two years ago, and had enjoyed several phone conversations with her since then.

Looking at the new TV in the corner and the new microwave in the kitchen, she smiled, hoping Amanda Carlson had enjoyed the benefit of the extra cash Erin had been depositing in her bank account since learning who she was.

"Please accept it as my gift to you—my small appreciation for giving me life," she had told Sassy, who had been reluctant to accept the money.

"Well, I guess there's a few things I could use around here," Sassy had finally relented. "Thank you, Erin."

A knock on the door broke the solitude. Sergeant Ken Tandry and another officer had arrived to discuss their findings about Sassy's murder with her only known living relative.

Erin took her bag into the spare bedroom, not looking beyond the closed door of the room where her mother had been gunned down. She was grateful that a restoration agency had already cleaned and repaired the room, so that one day when she was ready, she could more easily walk into the place where her mother had drawn her last breath.

Walking to the door to let Sergeant Tandy in, she told herself that Carlos would never think to look for her here.

CHAPTER SIX

Legacy of Love

THE NEXT WEEK WAS A BLUR OF ACTIVITY AS ERIN WORKED ON FINALIZING Sassy's affairs. Since no funeral had been planned, she spoke with an excavator about her idea to build a permanent tribute to her mother. They discussed the costs and logistics of bringing in an assortment of large mountain rocks that would be placed in a pile in the middle of the field. Around them would be arranged large pieces of concrete pipe—each about 6 feet in diameter and ranging from 4-6 feet tall, which would be placed with the ends upright and then filled with fresh potting soil. In three of the concrete planters, trees would be planted—healthy weeping birches. In two others, apple trees for the horses. For the remaining five planters, she envisioned an assortment of annuals and perennials. Hopefully, the work could begin by the first of June—Sassy's birthday. When finished, the garden would stand as a permanent memorial to her mother, right here on the small ranch her mother loved.

She exercised the horses daily, too, after finally teaching herself to abandon years of riding English to ride in the western style to which the horses were accustomed. She even enlisted the help of Sassy's students with this. As she honored their contracts with their instructor, she added her own flair by teaching them all she knew about English riding.

The students loved her as much as they had loved Sassy, which made it all the easier for Erin to decide to stay in Palmer indefinitely. When her parents arrived a couple of weeks later, they were more than impressed with the work their daughter had done, eventually flying back home to Santa Barbara with firm plans to return to Palmer that summer. By then, Erin planned to have

Sassy's room completely remodeled to suit her own taste, including installing a closed deck that would be accessible only from inside, and she would build a guest cottage for her parents.

Erin had ignored the several attempts Carlos had made to call her. She had walked away and never looked back from the minute she learned he was married. For one full year she had lived the high life in Mexico City in the apartment they rented together, never suspecting that he had a wife.

"Carlos Luis Antoya is a pig!" Imelda Antoya had told her over lunch that afternoon in the La Zona Rosa district of Mexico City after finding her number on Carlos' cell phone, putting two and two together, and confronting her husband's young lover.

Erin had been contrite in insisting she had no idea that the man she had been living with was married. His lengthy absences had always been explained as necessary business trips by the man who presided over several highly successful export companies. The fact that he was nearly twenty years her senior only intrigued her, and she never questioned or doubted the purity of their love.

"Do not be fooled into thinking that you are either the first or the only lover, Miss De la Corte," Imelda had told her. "Like his loyalty and morality, the passion of Carlos Antoya knows no boundaries. You would be wise to separate yourself from his clutches before he pulls you into the sordid reality that is his life."

"Why do you stay?" Erin had asked her.

"Such is the way of love," Imelda had replied.

CHAPTER SEVEN

Past Liaisons

WHEN ERIN FINALLY FOUND TIME TO RESPOND TO THE MESSAGE FROM Ellie on Sassy's answering machine, the conversation was pleasant and supportive, with Ellie at first expressing amazement that Sassy had been able to conceal the existence of an adult child all this time, but then warming to what she described to Erin as her "gentle persona."

The next day when the two women met for lunch in Palmer, Ellie told Erin that she was immediately struck by the close resemblance she bore to her birth mother.

"Your eyes are her eyes," Ellie said, "They were one of your mother's best features. And her hair was naturally blond, like yours."

A strange mixture of emotion rose within Erin at hearing Ellie talk about her mother. After all, she had grown up never knowing that anyone except Monica De la Corte was her mother. And she didn't look like her parents, a fact that had often puzzled her.

Unlike herself, Monica De la Corte was olive skinned with dark, curly hair that she wore tied loosely at the nape of her neck, and which she casually twisted up into a chignon when the occasion called for a more formal presence. Erin's parents were both short in stature, whereas Erin was quite tall. Her father, Angus, sported a burly frame that made him an imposing figure even though he barely stood at a height of five foot eight inches. Monica, as women of society somehow always seemed to be, was thin with refined features, while Erin always seemed to be fighting a battle to maintain her ideal weight.

"Your real mother had a colorful past," Ellie told her. "But, in the end, she proved herself to be a woman of substance and integrity, and of that you should be proud."

"I appreciate you bringing my mother's clothes down to me," Erin said while hugging Ellie at the end of their visit, "and I look forward to seeing you again."

Later that afternoon she gathered her mother's things into piles to be taken to the secondhand store in town. What a supportive environment she had found here in Palmer—at least judging from the people she had met so far. If she saw the fresh tire tracks in the dirt in the driveway and the large footprints leading around the house, she paid them no mind.

After deleting three more messages from Carlos from her phone, she went about the business of caring for the horses and then spent the rest of the week finishing the winter's riding lessons before flying back to Santa Barbara to spend a few weeks with her parents.

When she returned in early April, she would settle into a new life in this place known as the Butte, outside Palmer—a decision that invigorated her after dealing with the stress of her breakup with Carlos and the death of her birth mother. It was almost as if she was finding her roots—not that she in any way wanted to forget the wonderful life Monica and Angus De la Corte had given her. But here she could connect with the essence of her real mother, maybe even learning a bit about herself in the process. Perhaps it was part of the healing process. Whatever the case, she embraced the change it would bring in her life—or as Monica had put it, "a new opportunity for growth."

The new alarm system she had installed would keep the property safe in the interim—that, and the frequent presence of her students, who would be taking turns feeding and watering the horses under the supervision of Stan, the elderly ranch hand her mother had hired to help out with the ranch.

Meanwhile, up Knik River Road, Ellie Williams was busy sending extra supplies out to Ben Donaley, who had called explaining that—because of the uncertainty of knowing when the herring would come in—he would not be able to fly back from Sitka and pick them up himself.

Ellie mentioned that conversation in passing while having dinner up the road at Sarah and Ken's place a few days later. Since Ben said he didn't mind, she told Ken that a couple of IPA agents could stay up in the bunkhouse at her place while they were in town. After all, they would more than likely be finished with their work and gone by the time Ben got back, and so it should work out nicely all the way around and give her some extra security around the homestead as well.

Recently, she had been using the bunkhouse to house Ben until he could find a place of his own on the sparsely populated road she lived on—the only road that led up the south side of the Knik River to Knik Glacier. Dan had originally built the small apartment next to the stable so his brother would have a place to stay that afforded him some privacy when he visited from Homer. It had been Doug and Mara's idea for her to offer use of the quarters to house Ben Donaley since they were planning on being away fishing for much of the summer. Doug had often told her that he felt better knowing that there was someone around to help her out if needed, and this seemed like a perfect way to allay those concerns.

"Nothing in there that really matters," Doug had told her. "Tell your pilot to make himself at home."

CHAPTER EIGHT

Countdown

"KING MAN TO *THE WANDERER*. KING MAN TO *THE WANDERER*," BEN Donaley's voice squawked over the VHF that sat on the bridge of the *Fire Ring Roamer*.

Recognizing the code name for his seiner, Doug responded, "I copy, King man. See anything out there yet?"

"Affirmative, *Wanderer*. There's a small herring mass moving southeast off the tip of Little Mites Island, and what's shaping up to be another huge mass moving in not far behind 'em."

"We'll be moving out within fifteen minutes," Doug answered.

"Take 'er to plan B coordinates…plan B coordinates *Wanderer,*" Donaley squawked over the VHF again.

"*Wanderer* copies, King man."

"Once you're there, put 'er at one o'clock in Zone 8…repeat…Go to plan B coordinates and one o'clock in Zone 8."

"*Wanderer* copies, again, King man," Doug barked into the radio. Turning to his crew he said, "Donaley says there's a huge herring mass coming in off the southeast tip of Chichagof Island and he wants us to move to plan B coordinates, one o'clock position in Zone 8. Fish and Game just announced that the fishery will be opening any day now with as little as two hours' notice."

Jason Kent, Paul Hanson, and Mara all instantly understood the instructions, having spent much of the past week setting up and learning the system of codes they would be using. It was Mara who had come up with calling

Chichagof Island *Little Mites Island*. "It sounds like it was named after a tick or a chigger," she told them.

The rest of the crew, being from Alaska, weren't all that familiar with the insect species, but they went along with the captain's wife's wishes, and so the name stuck.

Fishing began in earnest around 6 p.m. that day when the whistle sounded for the first round of fishing after giving everyone only ninety minute's notice. Paul Hanson displayed his usual expertise in operating the jitney when in the first haul, Doug and his crew brought in a net so full that the crew had to use brailers to off-load enough fish to lighten it so it could be pulled up with its load. Working quickly, they scooped the fish out of the net, and with the use of an auxiliary winch, dumped them bucket by bucket into the hold, while the *Roamer* listed heavily to one side under the weight of the full net.

The next three days were several repetitions of the first with excited buyers deeming the quality of the roe to be superior, and paying top prices for the catch. Few, if any fishermen were failing to pull their full capacity in fish and aside from a near collision between two spotter planes, the usual organized chaos of the fishery went on without incident.

Mara had taken to the sea with a fervor that surprised even her. She relished her role on the bridge, taking the wheel of the *Roamer* sometimes to give her husband relief, and other times manning the radio or coordinating maps with Ben Donaley, who had turned out to be a skilled and effective spotter.

When Doug doubled over in pain after the net had gone out on the last set of day 3, Mara quickly took over controlling the boat while radioing for help for her husband. With nets in the water, she had no choice. Although they were fairly close to shore in the center of Sitka Sound, the Coast Guard opted to send over a chopper to take Doug to the hospital. With so many boats in the water, it would have been too dangerous to try to navigate a skiff—especially if the whistle sounded to start fishing. Having heard her distress call, two other boats came near, each sending one crew member over in dinghies to help keep the *Roamer* from capsizing or tangling in the nets, even in spite of the skills of Paul in maneuvering the jitney.

When the Coast Guard sent word from the hospital that Doug's diagnosis was appendicitis, Mara gave the okay for emergency surgery. Torn between wanting to be with her husband and the need to stay with his boat to protect their very livelihood, she forced her mind to stay focused and calm as she took command of the seiner.

How Derrk Stanley ever got on board in the tossing motion of the sea,

Mara would have trouble remembering hours later as she stood at her husband's bedside, but for right now she was beyond grateful that he and a crewman named Steve from a second boat had made their way aboard. They told her similar stories. Doug Williams was a friend to all in need and there wasn't any among them who would hesitate to help him out now or in the future.

Hours later, with all the fish off-loaded, the jitney secured, and the nets stacked on board, Mara, with the help of Derrk Stanley, guided the *Fire Ring Roamer* back into Sitka Harbor, leaving Paul and Jason to clean up. There would be no more fishing this season, she told them, but with the catch already being more than they had hoped for, she was certain that Doug would pay them their full wage plus a little extra for doing such a great job.

When she got to room 8 at Sitka Community Hospital, Doug was sound asleep in his room with an IV dripping through a needle secured in his lower left arm.

CHAPTER NINE

Storm Warning

"SOUNDS LIKE YOU DID A FINE JOB HANDLING HER," DOUG TOLD MARA when he woke up the next morning. "Wish I could have watched you."

A knock on the door, followed by a hearty hello from Derrk Stanley, made them both look up.

"Doug you old fish wrangler—how in the blazes did ya end up planning your appendicitis attack to happen just after ya made yer limit in fish?"

"Derrk," Doug said, trying to sit up to shake Derrk's hand, but forced down by the pain in his belly. "Tell Tom thanks for lendin' ya to help out Mara and the crew. Hope it didn't affect Tom's catch."

"Not at all, Cap," Derrk said to the man he had fished with for several seasons before signing on with Tom Bendle and his seiner last year when Doug didn't fish.

"Well, tell Tom it's much appreciated and I'll tell him myself soon as I get outta here," Doug said.

"Lucky I was nearby when ya needed me. Mara here was doin' a fine job of managin' the *Roamer* and yer crew was doin' a bang-up job holdin' the net steady in spite of that break in the cable you got to your Puretic power block."

Derrk glanced at Mara before continuing, "No tellin' what woulda happened if that cable had snapped when it was pulling fish instead of later when we were just stacking the nets. As it was, we were lucky to have laid most of the net on deck when it did snap. One thing's fer sure, your wife, Mara here, would never have had the strength that all us men together needed to pull the tip of the net back up over the deck rail before it could unravel the whole thing and pull it into the water when it broke loose. If that net would've kept going, no telling if it might have taken her or possibly one of your crew with it."

Doug was trying to sit up again and his brow was deeply furrowed, while

Mara listened in disbelief that she had been that close to danger and never even realized it.

"That cable—all the cables—were in top shape when we left Homer," Doug said. "I personally checked them all."

"Nobody but you coulda ever convinced me of that, Cap," Derrk answered. "But I'm here to tell ya that the cable above the I-bolt at the top of your Puretic power block was hacksawed about three quarters of the way through—climbed up there and eyeballed it myself—and you were darned lucky it didn't snap under the weight of the fish. No telling who coulda been hurt out on the deck or what kind of damage to the boat might have happened if that load of fish had dropped."

The pain medication the nurse had just given Doug was beginning to take hold and he let himself give way to its effects while Mara stroked his forehead lightly.

He fell asleep hearing the sound of his wife's voice thanking Derrk for all his help and midway through Derrk's response: "The pleasure's all mine, Mrs. Williams. Tell Cap I'll look in on him later in the week and we'll talk some more about goin' over the *Roamer* to make sure everything's okay before you two head out again."

On his way out the door, Derrk said to Mara, "Your crew…ain't no chance either of 'em…" Stopping himself, he let his voice trail off. "Just tell Cap I'll be talkin' to him."

———

Mara walked to a nearby café for some lunch while her husband slept. Afterwards, she walked into town and around St. Michael's Cathedral toward Katlian Street, stopping to look at the memorial to the family of Joe Michael, before turning and heading back to the hospital.

It had been here in Sitka where she had first discovered who the stranger really was who had given her a feather on the ferry when she first set sail to Alaska. Now, like his family, Joe Michael was gone, too—reportedly suffering from cardiac arrest at the very moment that her own life had been spared when Sassy had shot her brother, A.C., just as he was about to kill Mara. The two events had been more than coincidence, of that she was sure—and she would make apologies to no one for holding onto that belief.

It all seemed so long ago now, yet it had actually been less than a year. Now, with a posthumous warning from Joe Michael—not just for herself, but also for Doug—she feared that the nightmare that had been her life since arriving in Alaska—the nightmare that she had been so sure her marriage to Doug had cast into the dreadful past of bad memories—was not yet over. Two fouled fuel pumps and a hacked cable. She prayed that Doug would heal soon—before anything else happened.

CHAPTER TEN

Santa Barbara

ERIN DE LA CORTE WALKED INTO THE ATRIUM OF HER PARENTS' HOME in Santa Barbara, wondering why it was filled with at least fifteen bouquets of fresh flowers. One by one she read the attached cards, feeling her throat tighten and furrowing her brow as she did.

Erin, my love…call me—Carlos
Each flower pales when compared to your beauty—Carlos
Hoy, Mañana y Siempre—Carlos

She stopped reading after the third card. Something about his words for *today, tomorrow, and always* in Spanish made her cringe. Carlos seldom spoke Spanish in her presence, especially since he knew she did not understand it. In the times when he had, his voice had seemed to take on a barking, even angry tone that frightened her.

The sound of someone walking into the room brought Erin back to the present.

"Day by day, as each bouquet fades, a new one arrives to take its place," Monica De la Corte said, softly stroking the petals of a rose in one of the arrangements.

"I'm so sorry, Mama," Erin said hugging her mother. "I wish I could make him stop."

"This Carlos," Monica said, "You no longer love him?"

"I learned he is married, Mama. His wife found me after seeing my phone number on his phone. We had lunch. Until then I had no idea. She warned me that he is a pig, yet somehow she still loves him. For her sake—and for my own—I chose to walk away."

"Perhaps you need to tell him…" Monica began.

"No, Mama," Erin interrupted. "It is better this way."

Turning to face the woman who had raised her and nurtured her and loved her since she was first handed to her by her birth mother, Erin said, "Mama, I love you. It pains me to ask this of you, but—please—refuse delivery of anything else from Carlos Antoya. And, Mama, never tell him where I am."

"Don't fret, my darling," Monica said, embracing her daughter and stroking her hair. "I will have the staff take care of it. Now let's go out to the stable and bring your father in for lunch."

Angus De la Corte was in the process of picking himself up from the floor where he had landed against a support beam for one of the horse stalls when his wife and daughter walked into the stable. One eye was swollen and blackened and blood trickled from a deep laceration on his lower lip. Crudely tacked to the beam just above his head was a note that read:

Carlos Antoya sends his greetings to Miss Erin De la Corte and her family, and looks forward to seeing you soon.

"Daddy! What happened? Who did this to you?" Erin demanded, while her mother went for a cloth to clean her husband's face.

"Two thugs in suits," Angus replied. "They spoke to me only with the butt of their guns."

"But why? What could have been their reason?" Erin said, crying now.

"They spoke to each other only in Spanish," Angus told his daughter. "I couldn't make it out. They wore kerchiefs tied around their faces that muffled their voices."

"We must call the authorities," Monica De la Corte said, as she returned and dabbed her husband's swollen lip with a damp washcloth.

"They are long gone," Angus answered.

"Perhaps not so far," Monica replied. "The top drawer of our armoire was open when I went into the bathroom for the washcloth. The box with all of Erin's letters to us was gone."

"They obviously do not know you are here," Monica said to her daughter. "But I'm afraid they now know you have been to Alaska."

By now Angus was standing, and although wobbly, walking toward the door.

"I don't know who this Carlos is that you got mixed up with, daughter, but it'll be over my dead body that he gets anywhere near you again. Get the car, Monica, I'm going to talk to Don Shepherd."

"But Angus..." Monica pleaded, knowing all the while that her husband would not be deterred from visiting his friend, the local sheriff.

CHAPTER ELEVEN

Suspicion

ERIN WAS MORE THAN A LITTLE SHAKEN AFTER SEEING HER FATHER roughed up by Carlos' thugs. Why had they hurt him in the process of stealing information about her when they had obviously found what they were looking for while her parents were not even present in the house? The answer, she feared, was one she didn't want to think about.

Imelda had tried to warn her about Carlos. Erin had even already admitted to her mother that seeing the messages from Carlos in Spanish brought out uneasiness and even a fear inside her. Never, though, had she seen any actual evidence that Carlos could stoop to this level of violence until now. Perhaps it was time to take off the rose-colored glasses and see Carlos' true colors—a palette that held not only the green hues of jealousy and infidelity, but a disturbing personal spectrum of the colors of violence, greed, and revenge.

She was relieved that she had not shared her Alaska address with anyone. Instead, she had wisely chosen to use general delivery in Palmer for her mail, which was being forwarded via a mail service from Mexico. Since no one in Palmer besides Ellie Williams knew who she was, she felt secure enough to schedule a flight to Alaska for the next day.

"Imelda Antoya was right, Momma. Carlos is a pig," Erin said as they waited for her flight at LAX. "I don't want to have any further contact with him after what he did to Daddy. Will he be all right—Daddy? How can you both be safe in Santa Barbara now that this has happened and Carlos has found out where you live?"

Erin was becoming increasingly upset at the thought of leaving her parents alone. They were gentle people—not used to a world of violence and betrayal.

"I'm so sorry I brought such harm to you both, Momma. Carlos only did this to get to me because I'm not returning his calls. Maybe I should call him and beg him to stop."

"Calling him will only make him feel he can control you, Erin," Monica told her daughter.

"But he might try to hurt you or Daddy again…"

"You must resist the urge to contact him, Erin. He is much more dangerous than you believe him to be. Don Shepherd has already notified the FBI and the IPA of the attack because Carlos is a citizen of both Peru and Mexico, and the attack happened on U.S. soil. Apparently your friend Carlos, in addition to being married, has deceived you in other ways."

Erin paled and furrowed her brow as a chill ran through her at hearing her mother's words.

"What do you mean, Momma?"

"I mean that he is no good, Erin. He has lied to you on every level."

"But I trusted him. He said he loved me. He had business credentials. I saw them…" Erin spurted.

"They were only a front for his real activities," Monica told her daughter. "According to Don Shepherd, an agent from the IPA told him that Carlos Luis Antoya has been under surveillance by authorities in connection with an international drug cartel for over five years—"

"No!" Erin interrupted her mother. "It's not possible. I would have known something—heard something—no way, Momma. He's a very successful businessman. Carlos loved me. I left him only because of Imelda."

"Erin. You have always been a trusting and a loving person. Ever since the day I first took you into my arms, I sensed your gentleness."

Monica De la Corte gazed fondly at her daughter. Erin had become a fine woman whose undisciplined beauty bore an uncanny resemblance to her birth mother's, yet she possessed none of the haughtiness one would expect from someone of her social standing and looks. She and Angus had done a fine job of raising the child they had adopted to love. A tender smile momentarily softened Monica's already gentle face before being replaced with the furrowed brow of concern. "Someone who loves you does not stalk you—or try to hurt you by assaulting your family. I want you to have a bodyguard, Erin."

"A bodyguard, Momma!"

"Your father and I insist. We will pay all expenses. As a matter of fact, Don Shepherd has already assigned his own son to the case. You may remember meeting him at our Christmas party three years ago—Ethan Shepherd."

"I remember him, Momma. Tall and quite handsome if I have him right. He was studying at the police academy."

"That's him," Monica said. "He has since graduated and is now working undercover in Santa Barbara. Don pulled him off assignment and he will be in Palmer when you arrive. You are supposed to meet him at the police station in Palmer as soon as you arrive this afternoon. Authorities there will confirm his identity."

"Momma, do you really think this is all necessary?" Erin asked.

"I do and your father does, daughter," Monica replied. "Ethan will know what to do. I only ask that you listen to him and do as he says."

"But what about you and Daddy?" Erin asked her mother.

"We will be leaving for our villa in Costa Del Sol tomorrow. Don Shepherd does not believe we are in any more danger. He believes that Carlos delivered his message to you and that you are his real target."

"But, why?" Erin said, her voice a mix of fear and disbelief. "Simply because I choose not to be his lover anymore?"

"That is where the danger comes in, Erin," Monica said gently. "That is what none of us know. Promise me that you will listen and do as I say. The only reason we are going ahead with our visit to Spain is so that we do not look like we are disrupting our schedule in view of what happened. Believe me, I will be counting the days until we return."

Erin stood staring at her feet, trying to absorb all that had transpired in the past few weeks. Why was this happening? What was real and what was not? After several moments, she looked up at Monica De la Corte and said the words that would ease her mother's pain, "I promise, Momma."

42

CHAPTER TWELVE

Return Plan

WHEN ELLIE PICKED UP HER PHONE, BEN DONALEY WAS AT THE OTHER end. "I'll be coming in sometime tonight."

"I'll need to move the two men out of the bunkhouse that I've been letting use it," Ellie replied, not bothering to explain further.

She knew that Ben had a clear understanding that the bunkhouse was not for his sole use. He had told her more than once that he appreciated the locked storage room she had provided for him in the hangar.

"I'll use a cot in the storage room you loaned me in the hangar," Ben answered. "That space heater in there is all I need."

The rest of the news would have to wait until he saw her in person. Maybe by then he would be able to figure out exactly what spin he would put on things so she wouldn't be frightened. He hoped Mara or Doug hadn't called her yet. It didn't sound in talking to her, like they had.

He'd already talked to Ken Tandry, who had assured him that there was plenty of room for both Ellie and Anna up at their place, and that a visit would be more than welcome with Sarah now in the last trimester of her pregnancy. Convincing Ellie to go up there was the part Ben hadn't figured out yet.

"I'll leave a couple of warm blankets in the hangar for you," Ellie told him. "And a crockpot full of moose stew on the workbench in case you're hungry."

Ellie hung up and finished folding the load of Anna's clothes she had just taken out of the dryer. She hadn't heard from either Doug or Mara since learning that Doug had had an emergency appendectomy and was doing fine. They were probably busy getting the *Roamer* ready to return to Homer. She would ask Ben about them when she saw him tomorrow.

Two days earlier, Ben had been faced with the reality that would change everyone's plans much sooner than he had anticipated, when an unexpected encounter had thrown his stay in Sitka into turmoil.

"Benton! Benton Edwards, you old son-of-a…" a man's voice boomed from behind the table where Ben sat eating breakfast with Doug and Mara one morning

"Why I haven't seen you since Bunker ran that surprise touchdown that Paul, threw to him at their senior homecoming game."

"You must have me confused with…" Ben said to the tourist standing behind him, but not before Mara—pale with disbelief—grabbed her husband's hand and bolted from the table.

"Mara! Wait!" Ben shouted, taking off after them. "Doug! Let me explain."

Mara didn't want an explanation. She didn't even want this to be happening. Brad had told that story to her a million times—even laughing at how he had then been know by his teammates as *Bunker*. She had even met Paul once when the team had gotten together for an alumni reunion at their school. Now it all made sense—that eerie feeling of familiarity she felt every time Ben Donaley was near. There was no mistaking the truth. Ben Donaley was Benton Edwards, her deceased husband's father.

"Is nothing real anymore?" Mara screamed at Ben when he caught up with her. "Brad told me you were dead. Maybe you are dead. Maybe you're not who you claim to be…"

Ben took her by the arm and whirled her around, neatly avoiding a lunge executed by Doug, designed to take him to the ground.

"Let go of her," Doug railed against the affront, starting for Ben Donaley again.

This time Ben let go of her arm. "Hear me out, Mara…Doug."

Gently, Ben guided the three of them outdoors, away from the stares that had followed Mara's screams and Doug's subsequent outrage.

Something made Mara listen and her calmness made Doug listen, too. "That tourist was right. I am Brad's father and, no, I'm not dead."

Reaching into his breast pocket, Ben pulled out a crumpled picture of Brad and Mara. Immediately she recognized it as one a friend had taken right after they had arrived in Brazil. Ben handed her the picture, turning it over to show her the note written on its back:

> Dad, we're married! Can you believe how beautiful she is?
> I'll call soon. ~ *Brad*

"Like Brad, I worked for the IPA. I still do," Ben told them. "Like Brad's plane 'accident' my death was also faked."

Sadness overcame Ben's face as he continued, "I never thought my son would actually die—really die—like he did four years after his fake death."

For several minutes, no one said anything, each pacing around outside, yet none of them trying to leave.

Mara was the first to speak. "And your wife—Brad's mother?" she whispered.

"She died of natural causes last year. Brad was able to see her before she died. He and I—we always kept in touch. There's a secret island that the IPA owns. We would try to meet there at least once a year."

Ben stopped talking, watching the stunned faces of Doug and Mara, letting the words he had spoken sink in.

After another long silence, Doug spoke. "But why are you here? At Ellie's?"

"The IPA has reason to believe that Sassy's murder was somehow connected to the Mexican drug cartel. Our information is that A.C. was in possession of a large payment from his contacts in Canada, and that the Mexican cartel had recently learned he had double-crossed them by also working for the Brazilian cartel.

The Mexican cartel wanted their money before A.C. diverted all or some of it to the Brazilian cartel—something they suspected he had been doing for some time, but A.C. died before he could reveal the location of the money which they assume he put in the vault they—the Mexicans—had sent him. The thing is, our intelligence is that no one knows where the vault is hidden, or even if the money is inside it."

"Do you think Sassy was involved?" Doug asked.

"We don't think so," Ben answered, "but we think they do. We think they believe that Sassy was A.C.'s link to the Brazilians through Steve Bitten—not only because she was A.C.'s sister, but because of her personal relationship with Steve Bitten."

Ben stopped to give Doug time to digest what he was saying, staring at him, trying to measure the effect his words were having.

"As you learned right before he was killed, Steven Bitten was really my son, Brad, working undercover for the IPA. Our intelligence tells us that the Mexicans are working in the Palmer area in an attempt to uncover the location of the vault, and we—" Ben hesitated before continuing, "—and we have reason to believe that they will stop at nothing to find what they are looking for, even if that includes threatening anyone who ever knew A.C.—or, as it was in Sassy's case—even worse."

Ben paused again and then continued.

"That's why I'm here, to avenge my son's death and get these murderers locked away before they hurt anyone else. That, and in doing so, to make sure that you, Mara—and you, Doug—remain safe now that Brad is no longer here to protect you."

"All that time, I never knew he was protecting me," Mara whispered.

Doug stared at Ben Donaley. Either he was a very good liar and a very good actor or what he said made sense. The facts coincided perfectly with all he and Mara knew about that horrible day at Ellie's homestead when A.C. had shot Brad, threatened to shoot Mara and had ultimately been killed by Sassy in her desperate attempt to stop the carnage.

"I think we need to trust that Ben is telling us the truth, Mara," Doug said to his wife as she nodded in silent agreement.

He then proceeded to fill Ben in on the suspicious set of occurrences that had befallen his seiner, telling him that he never suspected it was anything more than pranksters or possibly some criminal element acting alone.

"Now," he told Ben, "I'm not so sure."

"I don't blame you for wondering if you should trust me after all that's happened," Ben said, "but I'm glad you have chosen to believe me. With everything that's gone on and with new intelligence coming in, your lives depend on it. I want you two to find another way home. Let your crew take your seiner in."

"But—" Doug protested.

"I can't stress to you strongly enough that your lives may well be in danger, "Ben continued. "I can almost guarantee it. Do you have another way home—some way that no one would know about?"

"We do," Mara answered. "Only one person would know and he's dead now."

"Well, he and his friend," Doug told her, reminding Mara about the man who had handed him his ticket to the ferry.

"Make arrangements to get your crew sailing with the seiner, and if possible, try to make it look to anyone outside your own crew like you are on board."

Doug trusted that Ben was right. He would have the crew take his and Mara's bags aboard the *Roamer* just before dawn, telling them he and his wife would need to stay in Sitka for another week for a post-op checkup. Meanwhile, he and Mara would leave on the ferry *Matanuska* which was scheduled to sail that afternoon.

"I have a plan," he told Ben.

"Godspeed, son," Ben said, his eyes watering as he gently slapped Doug's shoulder in that way that men do.

"Brad loved you, Mara," Ben said, looking at her—stopping himself from embracing her in case anyone was watching. "And he would have loved you, too," he told Doug.

"One last thing." Ben's voice took on a solemn tone. "No one but you two know who I am. No one. Ken Tandry knows I work for the IPA, but that's all. My life depends on you maintaining my cover. My life, and possibly both of yours."

The look on Doug's and Mara's faces told him they both understood.

CHAPTER THIRTEEN

A Weary Heart

Ben Donaley set the plane down on the long driveway that doubled as an airstrip on Ellie's property and taxied the Cessna to the hangar. The sun was just setting over Mount Susitna, creating the splendor of alpenglow that so often marked the coming of darkness over Alaska's snow-covered mountains. The light was coming back quickly now, making the days and nights just about of equal length. Soon it would be summer, and this same time of 6:30 p.m. would feel more like late afternoon, with dusk descending for only a few hours during the deepest part of the night.

He saw young Anna wave to him from the window and waved back. She was a delightful girl of about six and showed every indication that she would grow up to be as beautiful as her mother. He felt the anger rise in his chest—the same anger that always surfaced when he thought of the heartache and injustice and pain inflicted on innocent people like Ellie, Doug, Mara and even his own son at the hands of the cruel entity that was the international drug cartel he had been fighting much of his adult life.

He wondered now, as he had more often than not over the past year, if any of his work had been worth the sacrifices wrought on his personal life. Had he even made a dent in countering the efforts of the drug cartels? Slowed the pace of their operation one iota? Saved one innocent victim from the vengeful hands of the drug lords? At fifty-eight, he was growing tired of the chase. He longed for a more normal life, but his normal had been taken from him with the loss of his wife and then his son. Now he was an old man—alone—his future empty and predictable.

He fueled the plane, pushed the remote to open the doors to the hangar, and waited for the clunk at the end. He would talk to Ellie soon about having them adjusted for smoother operation. Right now, though, was not the time to trouble her about that. The doors were just one of several maintenance issues he'd noticed needed attention around the homestead. It was obvious that Dan Williams had built a quality operation, but with it now being close to a year since his death, things were beginning to fall into disrepair.

He hooked the cable from the power winch that was mounted inside the hangar to the plane and started the motor, slowing pulling the Cessna inside, disconnecting the cable and storing it when he was done before using the remote—this time to close the hangar doors.

A horse whinnied out in the yard and he instinctively grabbed his gun before hearing Anna's squeals of laughter and setting it back down. When he looked out, he saw her running with Thor while her mother fed the horses. The sight of them gave him courage and hope. For them he would keep fighting for justice. They had already suffered too much and he had nothing left to lose. At the same time, he tried to imagine the day when grabbing his gun would not always be the first thing on his mind.

"Take these in for your mother, would you please, Anna," he said, calling Anna over and handing the dirty dishes to the young girl, who seemed eager to help. "Tell her the moose stew was some of the best I've ever had."

"I will, Mr. Donaley," Anna told him, skipping off toward the house.

Did Ellie smile in his direction before turning back to the horses? She probably heard him tell Anna that the stew was good. Whatever the case, it felt good to have that kind of spontaneous goodness around him. A man needed that—an old man especially so.

He unbuckled his gun holster and hung it on the locked door, laying the pistol on the bench near where he was working. Systematically, he went through the plane, checking the fluid levels, cleaning the interior, even wiping down the fuselage with a clean cloth.

When he was finished, he loaded extras for the next flight and inspected the propeller. He rubbed out a small nick with emery cloth and waxed over the leading edge just the way his flight instructor and best friend, Clancy, had taught him to do so many years ago. Then he climbed up and cleaned the windows with Pledge—another trick that his friend had shown him. He also checked the tires and the shocks, and then the emergency equipment, wondering why Clancy had forgotten that essential step that might have saved his life when he made the emergency landing on a mountainside over twenty years ago.

He made sure that the fire extinguisher was secured on the floor behind the front seats for easy reach, and checked to make sure that the survival kit, including rifle, ax, sleeping bags, flares, tool kit, and even duct tape were secure behind the baggage area. He paid particular attention to the EPIRB 406 emergency locator beacon and his small, personal 406 as well. He secured the fire-retardant webbing that he had installed to replace the heavier nonstructural aft bulkhead, smiling as he remembered how the inspector had accepted this uncommon weight-reducing strategy without requiring the necessary paperwork—knowing that he had provided a safe and fuel-saving alternative more suitable for the long flights inherent in Alaskan flying.

Once Ellie and Anna had gone inside and the lights in the house were turned off, he met with the two IPA agents who had been staying in the bunkhouse and updated them on the latest developments in Sitka. In the morning, he learned, they would be moving to a rental house about 2 miles up the road between here and Ken Tandry's place.

"There's been some activity at Sassy's place," one of them told him. "It looks like somebody's moving in."

He didn't ask for any details. He would read their report, along with any others, in the morning. For now, he just wanted to rest. Seeing his daughter-in-law so upset had affected him more than he realized. She had married his son not knowing about his secret life. He and Brad had talked about that so many times. Not only had she lost him once, but she had seen him gunned down in front of her. Now, when she had once again found happiness, he had come into her life, bringing with him more stress and uncertainty to her fragile world.

Sometimes he wondered why he had ever taken on a job like this. He thought it had been for the adventure. What he had learned though, was that it was happiness he would have preferred.

He took Brad's shotgun out from under the cot and wiped it down with a cloth before placing it back in the locked case under a couple of loose floorboards in the hangar. If it were the last thing he ever did, he would make sure that Mara Benson Edwards Williams would finally be able to live a life free from the uncertainty and sorrow that had marked it so far.

CHAPTER FOURTEEN

A Woman of Determination

ELLIE WOULD HAVE NO PART IN HONORING THE SEVERAL SUGGESTIONS that she and Anna move up the road to stay with Ken and Sarah. Surely Ben, Doug, and the others did not think she was either stupid or helpless, so what was behind the conspiracy to get her away from the homestead?

The suggestion that Sarah might need her if she went into labor was lame. She knew her sister better than that. If Sarah needed her, she was only ten minutes away. When Ben Donaley asserted that he would be making a lot of noise that might disturb her while starting repairs in the hangar, she answered, "Hammer all day and half the night, if you've a mind to, Mr. Donaley. The sooner things are back in good repair, the better as far as I'm concerned."

So—what, actually, was going on?

The fact that Ben Donaley had chosen not to move back into the bunkhouse puzzled her a bit, but she believed him when he told her he was fine where he was. When a board she walked across in the storage room Ben called his temporary home flipped up to reveal a shotgun while she was taking him clean linens, she confronted him.

"I don't have anything against guns, Mr. Donaley, but it seems to me that if you require a safe place to store your weapons, that you might ask for the key to the gun case that is right over there on the far wall. It's been empty since Dan died and there's more than enough room."

"It belonged to my son," Ben told her; in what amounted to the only piece of truth he would deliver before ending with the lie, "He died in Iraq."

"I'm so sorry," she replied, feeling especially sympathetic when he pulled out a purple heart that he said was given to his son posthumously. In some strange way, perhaps keeping the gun near was helping him with his loss.

The gentle touch of her hand on his arm only served to intensify Ben's guilt at telling the lie, but the feeling was short-lived. He had learned long ago that to do his job well, no one could ever know the real truth about who he was.

"Well, at least he died a hero, huh?" Ben shrugged. "We didn't get along that well anyway, and I'm surprised he even told the army I existed. I'll lock the gun up in the case as soon as you give me the key."

"What about his mother?" Ellie pressed, trying to balance her concern for Ben's sadness with a need to respect his privacy.

"Mother?" Ben answered.

"Your son's mother," Ellie replied. "I take it she's no longer a part of your life."

"She ran off with some biker right after the boy was born. Never heard from her again until the divorce papers arrived five years later. Heard they both died in a collision with a semi a few years later—both high on drugs and playing chicken with the damned truck," he lied before stopping himself from carrying the deceit even further. "I apologize for my crudeness, Mrs. Williams. Guess I had more anger than I thought."

"It's okay, Mr. Donaley. Sometimes I feel the anger, too—but for reasons somewhat different from your own."

Ben was relieved that the conversation had finally shifted away from him and onto Ellie. He didn't like having to lie to a woman who was as kind and gentle as she seemed to be.

It was the first time since he had met Ellie Williams that he had heard her make any reference to her husband's murder, other than to tell him when she hired him that she was a recent widow and not to even consider taking advantage of that, which, she had added, was why she was hiring someone nearly old enough to be her father to fly for the business and serve as a hired hand.

"Well," she changed the subject abruptly, "I guess I'd better get inside and take care of helping Anna with her reading. She's been having a bit of trouble with one of the books in her study program, so every night we read a little bit together and talk about it."

"It's hard to believe that any book would be that hard for such a bright girl as Anna?" Ben said.

"The book's a bit advanced for her age, but it's a beautiful story about goodness. Perhaps you'd like to read it when we're finished?"

"Might be that I would," Ben answered, looking away before she could see the flash of gentleness in his eyes. "Guess I'll tend to those shrubs you asked me to trim."

Minutes later as he worked outside, Ben heard Ellie answer the phone.

"Sure, Erin, I can look for your mother's hair clip in the stable. I remember somebody saying they found one there after Dan—my husband—after he—well, anyway, I'll look."

"Everything okay?" Ben asked when Ellie came right out and headed for the barn.

"Yes, everything's fine," she told him, although the sad expression on her face said otherwise.

"That was Sassy's daughter—you know, the woman Doug dated before he married Mara—the one found murdered a couple of weeks ago in the Butte. She thinks her mother lost something in the barn…"

Ben Donaley's ears tuned out the rest of Ellie's words. None of the agents had ever mentioned hearing of Sassy having a daughter—or A.C. having a niece. Equally puzzling was the fact that Ellie Williams was acting as if it was common knowledge. How was it possible that no one from the IPA knew about this? How was it that he didn't know about it after living right here in Palmer?

Now he had no doubt that Ellie and her daughter, Anna, were in danger and he immediately updated the other agents working on the case. Tomorrow he would create a problem—cut a pipe to the house or something—to force Ellie to have to move out temporarily until he figured out just what was going on at Sassy's place, and before Ellie accidentally dropped this new information to the wrong person, whoever that wrong person might be.

CHAPTER FIFTEEN

Breaking News

BEN PLUNKED HIS CUP OF COFFEE DOWN SO HARD THAT A CLEAR BROWN splash flew across the workbench, just missing his laptop. He grabbed a rag to sop it up before scooting his stool closer to the edge of the bench where he anxiously clicked the *full story* link under the *Breaking News* article streaming across the top of his computer screen.

> AP 10 min. ago—A fishing seiner is burning in the Gulf of Alaska just west of Chichagof Island near Sitka. Several pilots in the area have reported hearing a loud boom and then seeing a large ball of fire. Other reports from vessels in the area confirm that the seiner is completely engulfed in flames. Two people have been spotted in the water and other boats in the area are moving toward them. Unconfirmed reports say that moments before the explosion, crew members aboard the seiner Fire Ring Roamer had placed a Mayday call, citing a fire in the main engine—This is a breaking news story. Stay tuned as more information becomes available.

"Thank God they got away," Ben whispered under his breath, just as he saw Ellie, looking pale and frightened, run from the house with Anna in tow.

"Turn on the news," Ellie called to him as she ran toward her car with Anna. "I've got to get to Sarah before she sees the news."

Then, as if making time stand still, she stopped and stared at him for a moment. When she spoke again, her voice had taken on an eerie calm. "I can't take this anymore," she said flatly. "It's like it's happening all over again."

Benton Edwards fought the temptation to ease Ellie's pain by telling her what he pretty much knew to be true—that Doug and Mara were somewhere else and not on the *Roamer*—but as an IPA agent known to her only by his alias of Ben Donaley, pilot/handyman, he concealed his real emotion.

"I saw the news. It's hard to believe it could happen," he said.

"I know that they had a few problems with the fuel pump and a couple of other things. I also know they had the seiner looked at by a mechanic," he told her.

Then, in an emotional move that surprised even him, he said gently, "I've got a feeling they're okay…Doug and Mara…I know they're your friends."

"You have to fly back to Sitka," Ellie said with a hint of impending hysteria in her voice. "You have to find them."

"Mrs. Williams…Ellie," Ben spoke, trying to keep his voice from revealing the pain he felt at seeing this fine woman face yet another loss. Hadn't she already been through enough in losing her husband in such a horrific way? "Won't do me or you any good to take off now. We need to wait it out. If they're okay, they'll let us know. Authorities are on the scene. Right now, we just have to wait while they do their jobs."

"But—" Ellie began before Ben interrupted her.

"Keep your wits about you, Mrs. Williams. I know that Doug had an appointment with his doctor scheduled for yesterday. That means there's a good chance they sent the boat out with just the crew and are probably safe somewhere in Sitka."

"I haven't heard from them in a week," Ellie said, her voice quivering. "All I get when I call is that their voicemail is full."

"You go on up and be with your sister," Ben told her. "It'll make you feel better—both of you—to be together until there is more news. You've got your cell phone and you can check your answering machine from Sarah's, right? If I hear anything at this end, I'll call you. Anything…"

———

Twenty minutes later, Ellie and Sarah sat glued to the television set in Sarah's living room. When the second news bulletin came on, they sent Anna outside to play.

> Breaking News—This just in: rescuers report that they have rescued two crew members from the waters surrounding a fishing seiner in Southeast Gulf of Alaska. The crew members have been identified as Jason Kent and Paul Hanson,

both of whom currently serve as crew aboard the fishing seiner Fire Ring Roamer based in Homer, Alaska. Early reports indicate that both men were thrown by the blast aboard the seiner into the icy waters of the Gulf of Alaska, but thanks to a rapid response by surrounding vessels, both are expected to survive. There is no word, yet, on the whereabouts of Captain Doug Williams and his wife, Mara, who were also thought to be on board the seiner when the explosion occurred. Reports from other vessels near the scene indicate that the seiner is burning uncontrollably in the Gulf of Alaska off the western edge of Chichagof Island, and that small oil sheen is burning on the water surrounding the vessel. Stay tuned for more information as it becomes available.

"What's wrong, Mommy?" Anna cried after hearing both her aunt her mother scream. When all either of them could get out through their sobs were the words, "Aunt Mara and Uncle Doug..." the young girl began crying, too.

Ben Donaley wasted no time contacting the two IPA agents who had been staying in the bunkhouse. He shared his suspicion that the fire on the seiner was tied up with several recent incidents of apparent tampering on the *Fire Ring Roamer*. He even disclosed that he had been forced to reveal his identity as an agent with the IPA to Doug and Mara when Mara had recognized him, and he finished by telling them he had advised both Doug and Mara to stay off the vessel while making it look like they were on board as usual. Where the two currently were, though, he did not even know himself, and thus was unable to tell them.

The call from chief investigating agent Karen Steele the next morning came as no surprise. When Ben met up with her for breakfast in Palmer, the look on her face told him all he needed to know.

"Doug and Mara—when we find them—they can never know about me—especially not now," she said quietly, making sure that no one could hear. "It would be disastrous to you, me, and them."

Ben's heart did a flip-flop in his chest knowing that Karen Steele was right. Mara trusted her—especially since Karen had revealed that her romance with Brad had been a sham and part of their undercover work under Brad's alias of Steve Bitten, to solve Dan William's murder.

"Brad has always loved you," she had told Mara in an emotional exchange that had somehow eased the shock of her finding Brad alive after four years of believing he was dead.

Since that time, Mara had found happiness again by marrying Doug and putting the past behind her. That is, until all the funny business with the seiner had surfaced, along with another mysterious note from Joe Michael, who she also thought to be dead—she and Doug had even attended his memorial service on a beach in Hoonah.

Now, just when normalcy had returned to Mara's life, her world had been shaken up again in learning that Ben Donaley was really Brad's father Benton Edwards—also an IPA agent and was another person she had long thought was dead.

"Any more news about people not being who they seem to be will surely blow any remaining trust Mara might have in any of us," Karen Steele said.

"I know, Beth" Ben said. "If Mara knew about you, no telling how she would handle the news and it could endanger both your cover and your safety. I lost your mother and your brother and I'm not going to risk losing you, too."

"Then don't ever call me Beth again until this is over—especially in public, Daddy."

CHAPTER SIXTEEN

Missing Captain

MARA WATCHED THE FIRE FROM THE DECK OF THE *KENNICOTT* WITH DOUG. This ferry was bigger than the *Malaspina*, on which she had first traveled to Alaska.

When a crew member heard her mention that to Doug, and said in passing, "This is one of the biggest ferries, you know," that was good news as far as she was concerned. The knowing look Doug gave her told her he agreed it would be easier to stay anonymous with more people on board.

"Ben Donaley was right about us being in danger," Doug said.

Standing along the deck with one arm around his wife's shoulders, he felt the shiver run though her body and pulled her more tightly to him as, expressionless, she stood watching their livelihood burn in the sea.

"Pretty big fire," another crewman said, while inspecting some ropes that were wound tightly around cement posts as thick as logs on deck.

Mara stared at the posts. They were huge. It made sense that they were so big—they needed to be to hold the ferry securely against the 20-40 foot tides that were the norm in Alaska. On some level, thinking of the tides brought to mind the series of extreme highs and lows that had marked the last five years of her life.

"Heard they got the crew out of the water, though," the crewman said, bringing her thoughts back to the present. "Sure was a relief to hear that. The captain's missing, though—and someone said his wife was, too. Real shame if you ask me. Heard they were newlyweds."

Mara paled at hearing his words. Sarah, Ellie and the others must be frantic. It was a feeling she knew all too well. Brad had been missing for four years before investigators had given up and declared him legally dead. As much as she didn't want their friends to have to go through the shock and uncertainty she had, she knew that she and Doug would have to keep their whereabouts—and even the fact that they were alive—secret for now.

"They must be worried out of their minds," Doug said, mirroring her own thoughts.

Mara didn't answer. Words were too trite to describe what she was feeling. Instead, she clung more tightly to her husband's arm.

'That trouble with the fuel pump—twice—and then the puretic power block—looks like they were no accident," Doug said.

Mara looked at him. Tears were welling in his eyes as he looked out over the water watching the *Roamer* burn. She turned away. Seeing his pain was too much to bear.

"There ain't gonna be nothing left of her…"

She fought back her own tears.

"Maybe it's a blessing in disguise that you got appendicitis," she told him." Otherwise, we'd be out there right now."

The words sounded empty—like trivial blather—even to her. The *Roamer* was Doug's lifeblood and had been for the last fifteen years. How many times had he told the story of how he had bought her from an old fisherman in Kodiak whose bad hips had persuaded him to retire?

"She's our future," he had often told her. "As much a part of us as the air we breathe."

For a moment, she stood there on the deck with the man who had become her anchor in life. Whatever they were up against, they would face it head-on—together.

"It's going to be hard not to let them all know we're okay," Doug said, again mirroring her own thoughts. "But something tells me we'd better heed Ben Donaley's advice and stay low."

Doug was right. Too many people close to them had died at the hands of the drug lords. Now for some reason, she and Doug were also in their crosshairs. Why?

She knew the answer. Brad. Brad—Dan—Sassy—A.C.—each of them, all of them, and each of their combined tragedies had to be the reason. She and Doug were just another two people who, in the minds of the drug lords, were guilty by association.

The others would have to believe she and Doug were missing in order for them to stay safe. Ben had warned them and knew they had a plan. Even he, though, did not know where they were. Jason and Paul, their loyal crew, were safe, but it would be only a matter of time before they would have to reveal to authorities that the captain and his wife had not been on board the seiner.

The lifetime ferry pass had come with a specially issued code that protected their identity from all but security elements for the ferry system. Mara was sure that they were as safe aboard the *Kennicott* as was possible. If it came up, to anyone who might ask, they would be Jane and Bob Brown of Oregon—here celebrating their fifteenth wedding anniversary by touring Alaska the way "real Alaskans" traveled. It was a plan she and Doug had agreed on.

———⌣———

When the *Kennicott* docked in Kodiak, Jane and Bob Brown checked into the honeymoon suite of a local bed and breakfast. Along with their room key, they received a complimentary bottle of champagne and heartfelt good wishes from their hosts, after which they retreated to their room.

Two days later they boarded the smaller ferry, *Tustemena*, to Dutch Harbor, where they stayed another two days. Close to a week after they had turned up missing, they departed once again on the *Tustemena*, this time for the Aleutian Chain.

By now Doug was sporting a healthy growth of beard and Mara had let her hair revert to its natural curl. She wore it long and flowing for the most part, although sometimes she wrapped it into a thick, long braid that hung down her back.

The two had long ago traded their lighter-weight clothing for heavy sweaters, thick canvas coveralls, and the knee-high rubber boots that made them indistinguishable from scores of other young couples that lived in the area.

Although it was risky, Doug had taken payment for his fish in cash, which he carried in a pouch chained to the belt loops of the jeans he wore under his wool bib overalls. He gave Mara half of the money, which she stashed inside her sports bra. As an extra precaution they each carried ten one-hundred-dollar bills inside their boots.

Doug and Mara were just two of many other semirecognizable faces around town who worked seasonal jobs in Alaska, lived a transient lifestyle, and who carried their money on their person and paid in cash—all of which made it easy for them to blend in.

Like most everyone else, they were fishermen, with no one seeming to notice that they didn't have a boat with them right now. Some even knew Doug by face, if not necessarily by name. Most of the people they came in contact with were busy working and didn't bother to read the mainstream news all that often. Trade papers and word of mouth were how they usually got the information pertinent to their lives.

Doug and Mara had little to fear here. Most direct contact with anyone came in the form of a nod at the store or across a beer in the local hangouts. And even if someone did recognize them, there was little chance they would have heard the news about the fire before the two were off to a new location— usually within a couple of days—after giving false information about where they were heading, just in case anyone happened to be interested.

CHAPTER SEVENTEEN

Ethan Arrives

WHEN ERIN DE LA CORTE MET ETHAN SHEPHERD AT THE STATE POLICE post in Palmer, the two exchanged pleasantries and briefly reminisced about the few times they had met while in high school. When they arrived at Sassy's place, they were met by the caretaker, Stan, who informed Erin that the alarm in the house had gone off two times while she was away.

"First time was around noon day after ya left," he told her, relaying that the second time was around 3 p.m., two days later. "Couldn't find nothin' amiss either time. I wanted to check with you before I called in the alarm company to see if there's a short or somethin'."

Erin thanked Stan for his diligence in watching the place, and informed him that he should proceed to set up an inspection by the alarm agency.

"Stan, this is my good friend Ethan Shepherd," she said in the way of introduction. "You'll be seeing a lot of him around here and feel free to share any information you want to with him." Erin winked and put her arm through Ethan's arm, feeling him tense slightly as she did.

"Don't worry, I know all about Michael," she whispered in Ethan's ear as they walked to the house, leaving Stan behind to tend to his usual duties.

"But, how?" Ethan said, clearly surprised that she knew about his relationship.

"Don't worry. Neither your father nor my father knows anything about Michael as far as I can tell. And, as far as anyone in Alaska is concerned, you and I are involved and you'll be living in my house as my boyfriend. No one has to know the truth that you are really my bodyguard."

Ethan had gone to great lengths to keep his and Michael's relationship a secret. With Michael's conservative father up for re-election as governor of his state this year, and with his own father in a position of prominence in his community, he had gone to great lengths to keep from calling attention to their choice to be together as a couple—even nurturing a reputation as a heartthrob by dating a string of attractive young women. The fact that he had run off to Alaska only added to his reputation as a heartbreaker, leaving at least two of his latest "girlfriends" to claw the truth about his true intentions out of each other.

The thought of it only added to the inner conflict that seemed to be ever present. He winced, remembering the words spoken by his father at his graduation from the police academy and right before he had received his first undercover assignment. The words that had hit him right in the solar plexus then, and were as distressing to him today as they had been the day they were spoken. "Proud of you, son," Don Shepherd had said. "You turned out to be one heck of a man."

Knowing that there was no way his own father would accept that his only son was gay had forced him into leading a secret life, and the fact that he had to hurt others in the process only added to his inner turmoil. One day, he would tell his father the truth and stop living the lie—but he just wasn't ready yet. After all, he had Michael to consider in all this, too, and Michael was even more private than he was.

"I always liked you as a person, Erin," Ethan told her. "Looks like that fact is going to come in pretty handy now that I need to trust you as much as you need to trust me."

Erin had been regularly checking her messages from Santa Barbara, happy that—except for the one from her mother saying that they had arrived safely in Spain and were enjoying the sun—there hadn't been any for several days, so it came as a bit of a surprise that the LED on her phone showed six missed calls. Scrolling through them, she noted that all but one of them said *private caller*. The sixth one, however, displayed the cell phone number she knew from memory—that of Carlos Antoya.

"What's wrong?" Ethan said, seeing the look of disbelief on her face.

"Somehow the person who I lived with for one year—the man who turned out to be married and whose wife told me was not to be trusted—has found this phone number," she answered, pointing out that she had changed her number just before leaving for Alaska this time.

"Ethan, this is the same person who left the note in the stable after my mother and I found my father lying there beaten. My mother said some papers with my personal information were missing from her armoire in Santa Barbara. With only one area code for the state, by now I'm sure he knows I'm in Alaska. What I don't know," she said, scowling, "is if he knows where in Alaska I am."

Ethan went outside to retrieve their bags and carry them into the house. He didn't like the sound of this already. First of all, why would anyone want to rough up a gentle man like Angus De la Corte, and secondly, why had Carlos deceived Erin about the fact that he had a wife, and why had that wife warned Erin to beware of her husband?

It was easy enough to dismiss the warning by Carlos' wife as a jealous comment by a wronged woman, but even so, to put it in the form of the sinister warning that Erin had repeated to him concerned him. And why would Carlos want to hurt Erin by hurting her father, who she obviously loved very much, unless he was actually trying to hurt her?

"Do you have reason to believe that this man, Carlos, would want to harm you?" Ethan asked Erin point-blank.

"Only that I left him and haven't returned his calls," Erin replied.

"No. I mean harm you—as in physically hurt you," Ethan said.

"I never really thought of that until…" Erin said.

She went on to explain that she had failed to return several voicemail messages to Carlos since walking away over a month ago from the apartment he had rented for her in Mexico City. She told Ethan that the messages had continued in spite of her ignoring them—even causing her to go as far as to change her phone number just before coming back up to Alaska.

"Last week when I got to my parents' house in Santa Barbara, the foyer was filled with over twenty bouquets of cut flowers from Carlos," she told him. "Mother said they had been coming in for weeks, always a fresh arrangement to replace those that had died."

"Was that unusual?" Ethan asked her.

"Yes. Why my mother's house? I hadn't told him I was there and I don't think I ever told him where they lived, "she answered.

"Did he say anything—send any messages with the flowers?" Ethan asked her.

"Just the usual types of romantic messages," Erin answered. "Except for the one written in Spanish that translated to 'today, tomorrow and always.'"

Walking across the room, she thought for a minute before turning to look at Ethan. "Carlos knows I don't speak Spanish, and I have never known him to use his native language in my presence unless he was angry with someone and didn't want me to know what he was saying."

"So, he never left you notes or love sentiments in Spanish?" Ethan asked.

"Never," Erin replied.

"And how did you feel when you saw the note in Spanish on the flower arrangement in your mother's home?"

"Frightened," Erin answered.

CHAPTER EIGHTEEN

The Blizzard

With Ethan's approval, Erin decided to sabotage Carlos' repeated attempts to call her by letting her voicemail remain full. She would monitor her caller I.D. for now and see if Carlos' calls continued.

After about a week, the calls from Carlos stopped. Hopefully, he had figured out that she was not using that account and so she turned her voicemail back on. After another week, when there had still been no more calls, she began to relax.

Monica De la Corte had just returned from Spain and had assured Erin that there had been no more flower deliveries. She shared Erin's sentiment that the attack on her father had probably been a spontaneous moment of jealous rage by her spurned ex-lover.

Ethan, though, told Erin he was not convinced that a man who had proven himself to be as violent as Carlos Antoya had just quietly given up on his yearlong relationship with her—especially in view of the cryptic words that had been delivered by Carlos' long-suffering wife, Imelda.

Also not convinced were Ethan's father, Erin's father, or the police departments in Santa Barbara and Palmer, thus prompting Erin to reluctantly agree that Ethan would remain as her bodyguard for the indefinite future—a decision his partner, Michael, although disappointed, was willing to accept in view of his experience with Ethan working undercover in the past. Now Ethan and Erin could begin living the life that for now would be their "new normal."

The sudden late March blizzard that descended on the area caught Californians Erin and Ethan completely off guard. Luckily Stan had a plow blade for his pickup, but even he grew weary after removing at first, 2 1/2 feet of snow, then another foot of snow, and then 2 inches of slush with 6 inches of wet snow on top.

By late in the day, a blizzard warning had been posted for 2-9 more inches of snow and for expected blizzard conditions overnight. Before Stan retreated to his room over the stables, he taught Ethan and Erin how to build a fire in the woodstove—making sure to leave enough wood stacked under the overhang outside the back door so they could stay warm if the power went out.

Because of the higher elevation of her homestead on the mountainside, conditions at Ellie's place were just as bad, if not worse than those in Anchorage and the Mat-Su Valley.

Ellie had chosen to move back down to her own house a few days earlier. "Look, I can't stay hidden away here forever," she had argued with Sarah, agreeing that she would move back in with her sister at the first sign of any trouble. When the snowstorm began, she told herself she was glad that she had come home. She wouldn't want to risk having the storm damage her property by not being there.

Ellie was glad that Ben Donaley hadn't found a house yet, and even invited him to stay in the guest room when the winds hit close to 90 mph, making it feel as though the roof might come off or the house collapse. Since it was too windy to burn the woodstove, Ben fired up the backup generator when the power went out, and the two of them spent the evening playing scrabble until long after Anna had fallen asleep. They spent the evening talking about everything from Dan's murder to Ben's stories about some of his exploits piloting bush planes both in Alaska and elsewhere.

When Ben found himself focusing too much on how warm and charming Ellie was, he yawned and made an excuse to turn in for the night. He was starting to like the way this woman, who had become a widow too young, was raising Anna, and the wonderful young lady the six-year-old had become—a sentiment that not only took him out of his comfort zone, but also brought back intense feelings of the loneliness his life had become.

Dan had hooked up the generator to run all of the home's essential appliances and had also set up a series of alarms to alert them if there were any problems with low fuel or malfunction. There was little need for Ben to worry about the family's safety for the night. Even so, he slept lightly, with his ear trained on the hum of the generator, so as not to miss any alarm that might sound.

By the time the storm was over, there were four more feet of snow on the ground, with much higher drifts blown up against the hangar doors, making it impossible to get the truck out to try to clear the area. Bit by bit he, Ellie, and Anna shoveled away at the drifts, slowly creating a path to the entry door and then along the front of the hangar.

It had been a calculated move on Ben's part to park the truck inside. The heavy snow would have buried it for sure. Once inside the hangar, he used the remote to open the doors, leading him to where he had deliberately backed the truck in before parking. For the next four hours he plowed until the yard was cleared enough for the plane to turn around in if he needed it to, and a path wide enough for his truck had been made all the way to the highway.

Meanwhile, Ellie had gone inside to make them all some warm food and Anna was building a snowman over near the house. As it was, Ben would need to work some more to widen the driveway after he rested, as the snow was so deep that the berms were higher than the plane's wingtips. But for right now, he gave Anna a hand with her snowman, before joining Ellie in the house for a hearty lunch.

When they were done, he filled his truck up with diesel from the storage unit on site just as he had done twice already that morning, and finished plowing. The gauge on the large fuel tank next to the hangar showed it was still three quarters full. Reassuring since, with the weather being this severe, the likelihood of a fuel truck getting in for the next couple of days was minimal.

The fuel oil tank next to the house was also nearly full, ensuring that the family would have plenty of fuel to get them by. Just in case, though, Ben stacked some extra wood by the front door while Ellie moved some of the furniture away from the woodstove so they could fire it up in a hurry should they need to.

Meanwhile, down in the Butte, Erin and Ethan took turns shoveling a path out from the house, while Stan worked the driveway and yard with his truck. There, too, the snow had fallen to a record 4 feet in depth, bringing everything in the area to a standstill. Only the distant roar of snowmachines and the hum of trucks plowing out drives broke the silence.

Since Erin didn't know how to cook, Ethan took over that task. Thawing some frozen chicken he found in the freezer and using some canned broth he found in the pantry, along with some of the goods they had brought with them from the store in Palmer, he cooked up a batch of homemade soup that Erin told him was the best she had ever tasted. Stan said he thought so, too, and they ate their fill before setting out to work on snow removal until nightfall.

CHAPTER NINETEEN

Back to Homer

HUDDLED NEXT TO HER HUSBAND, MARA STOOD BY THE DECK RAIL OF the *Tustemena* watching the heavy snowfall while the ferry slowly pulled away from the Seldovia dock. They had spent the better part of an afternoon in the small village, walking about town using the same narrow paths others had made while trying to get around through the thigh-deep snow.

The usually bustling village streets were empty—devoid of most of the trucks and four-wheelers people usually used to get around here. Trudging around the nearly deserted town had been their only choice unless they wanted to stay on the ferry, and after two days at sea they were ready for some time on land.

Most of the side streets had been nearly impassable. Like a few other hardy souls, they had tried to gingerly navigate steep berms and narrow paths that had been worn to a bumpy trail of hard-packed snow by those braving the elements to walk for supplies. Only the grocery store had been open, leaving them with little else to do but buy a frozen hamburger, heat it in the micro-wave that stood at the end of a counter facing the window, and watch more snow fall while they stayed warm and ate.

While there, they read the local paper twice, talked about nothing with a couple of other tourists, and felt grateful when the horn blast sounded for them to once again board the ferry. Once underway they took their places along the deck rail, watching the land shrink into the distance.

It was interesting how beautiful the water looked against the backdrop of the white curtain all around them. Even in nearly whiteout conditions, they could see jellyfish with their long tentacles, bobbing in the brilliant green sea as the ferry moved across the water with only the hum of its engines and the rhythmic click of the slowly rotating navigation antenna breaking the silence. In about 40 minutes, they would be in Homer and neither one of them was looking forward to that.

"I don't see any other choice, Mara," Doug said. "By now Jason and Paul must have revealed that we were not on board the *Roamer* when she went down, and I suspect the authorities are probably finding it kind of fishy that we suddenly turned up missing about the same time."

Doug put one arm around Mara and pulled her to him, kissing her lightly on the side of her face. "I think the best thing to do is to let out word around Homer that we think somebody sabotaged our boat, which is pretty much what happened as far as I can tell. There's enough folks around there that know the trouble I had with the engine before I left, to stand behind me on that assumption."

"But they don't know me so well," Mara said.

"They know me enough to know I'm gonna protect you," Doug told her. "I don't think anyone's gonna find it strange that I put you in hiding somewhere until things get figured out. The rest of it, though, I'm gonna have to talk to Ben Donaley."

"What about Ellie and Sarah?" Mara asked.

"I'll tell them the same thing I tell the folks in Homer—that you are visiting some old friends back East until I can get to the bottom of whatever's going on."

"That's probably going to scare them even more," Mara answered.

"All the more reason for them to understand why you need to be away," he replied. "We'll set it up so you call from this calling card in a couple of days to make sure they know there's nothing wrong between me and you, and also to give you a chance to convince them that you're okay—and that'll be the truth, Mara. You and I are both okay. That's why we're doing this, so we stay that way."

"What about the seiner? What will you tell them about that?"

"Just that we were having trouble both in Homer and in Sitka and that I'm cooperating with authorities to get to the bottom of it. Look, Mara, you know and I know that if anyone messed with me and the seiner, it has to be connected to what happened with A.C., Brad, and with Dan—especially now with Sassy being murdered. I can't risk losing you—not when it took me my whole life to find you."

They had spent last night in a hotel and both of them yearned for that privacy now, but with the Homer Spit in sight, they ducked into a dark hallway off the kitchen and settled for a passionate kiss and a lingering embrace before gathering Doug's things from the cafeteria, where he had stacked them in one of the booths.

"I think it's best if you make yourself scarce for now," he told her. "No sense calling attention to the fact that we were traveling together."

"I love you," she whispered later, as she saw him emerge clean-shaven from a nearby restroom and caught his eye before he started walking toward the line that was forming to unboard the ferry.

"I love you, too," he mouthed the words back, bending down to pick up his backpack off the floor to divert attention away from their interaction— just in case anyone had been watching.

"I know," she said in soft words directed at his back.

CHAPTER TWENTY

Visit from the Past

MARA WATCHED DOUG WALK DOWN THE GANGWAY WITHOUT LOOKING back. She knew that if he turned around to see her that he wouldn't be able to continue. *Please let her/please let him be okay*, their thoughts crossed. She watched him walk into the terminal from her place on the deck. She called out for him to stay safe, knowing her words had been unable to reach his ears.

"Love will hold you together if it's real," a man's voice said beside her. "And it will break your heart if it's not."

Startled, she looked up, only to see the bent form of an old man walking away. She knew that walk! She knew that ball cap and the tufts of gray hair sticking out from under it. When the man's head turned slightly sideways as he walked, she recognized the black-rimmed glasses.

"Joe Michael—stop!" she called to him, but he ducked into a side door before she could catch up with him.

Two hours later, the *Tustemena*, with Mara on board, was well on its way back to Seldovia. As hard as she tried—walking the perimeter of the decks at least three times, and even going down for a car deck call when she didn't even have a car—Mara could not find the man whose gift of a feather had saved her life, and who himself had been honored at a memorial service in Hoonah after his death had been announced on local TV around one year ago. But she *had* seen him and he was *not* dead, she knew that for sure—or at least she thought she did.

Locking herself into her stateroom, she cried harder than she had since the whole saga surrounding Dan Williams' death had unfolded. Was anything in her life real? She screamed skyward, demanding to know why life was doing this to her. Overwhelmed—she felt as though she might die from the burden of all the stress. She had been through a hell she thought was now over, but hell had returned with Sassy's murder, with discovering that Brad's father was still alive and, now, with the shock of learning that Joe Michael was not dead.

Wracked with sobs, she screamed at the wall, the floor, and she screamed at God, before throwing herself on the narrow lower bunk mounted just inside the stateroom door, where she buried her face in a pillow and screamed herself hoarse.

"Everything okay in there?" an official-sounding voice said after a gentle wrap on her door.

"Yes, I'm okay..."she tried to say in a normal voice. "I just...I just got some bad news. I'm sorry I caused a disturbance."

"Let us know if there's anything we can do," the voice replied. "Sure you're all right?"

"Yes, I'm sure. Thank you. I'm sorry. I will," she answered meekly. How could she have lost it like this—and in a public place?

Mara skipped dinner that night, and breakfast and lunch the next day. The ferry had stopped in Seldovia for only a few hours before continuing to Kodiak. With her eyes still swollen and red from crying, she forced herself to go to the cafeteria for dinner, telling her concerned waiter that she was simply suffering from allergies and could she please have the hot roast beef sandwich with mashed potatoes that was the special that night.

Later, while standing outside by the deck rail as the ferry rocked in the rolling seas, she heard footsteps and looked to see Joe Michael standing beside her.

"Sorry to frighten you," he told her, looking very much alive.

"But...but I thought you were dead," she stammered.

"Faked it," he answered in the same flat, monotonic accent that she remembered hearing when he had first handed her the feather.

"But it was on TV—the memorial—in Hoonah—the totem—the wind—the feather—" she rambled, staring at him in disbelief.

"Yeah. Lotta hoopla. Pretty believable, huh?" he chuckled.

"But how—" she started to ask.

"I know people," he answered, anticipating her question.

"But it seemed so real..." she stammered again.

"Yeah. They done good," he replied.

"But why?" she said, looking at him dumbfounded. "Why?"

"I got tired of all the BS," he answered. "Too much hassle—being a legend and all that. No one believes that stuff is real anymore."

"But I did," Mara told him. "You saved my life."

"You sure about that?" he answered with a twinkle in his eye.

"Yes!" she shouted, unamused. "I *am* sure about that."

"Just coincidence, Ms. Edwards—er—Ms. Williams," he said.

"How do you know my name then?" she demanded. "How do you know both of my names?"

"Oops," he answered before walking away and once again disappearing down a nearby stairway.

The sound of the door banging closed told her it had not been a dream.

CHAPTER TWENTY ONE

Sal

FOR THE REST OF THE TRIP, MARA THOUGHT ABOUT JOE. WHY HAD HE faked his own death? Was he simply, as he had told her, "tired of the BS," or was there something else going on that had caused him to appear in her life again? Certainly those who had mourned him in Hoonah had seemed sincere and his death had seemed real. Perhaps, as he had told her, he was tired of being a legend. She couldn't fault anybody for that.

How much impact had Joe's death, real or faked, had on anyone, really? Joe's family was gone, and aside from a few ferry workers who saw him come and go, and the couple of friends Doug had met in Homer, Joe seemed to live a solitary life. The ceremony could have simply been one of traditional respect for an elder—even if it was an elder that few people knew.

She could certainly appreciate the beauty that the anonymity of riding full-time on the ferry provided, now that she was doing just that herself. Ever since Joe had handed her the feather, she had learned to trust the old man and take his words to heart.

For whatever reason, whenever he appeared, she had always remained safe. The big question was, why was he here now? Especially after going to all the trouble to appear dead. She so wanted to believe that this meeting had been simply by chance and was not a sign of more troubles heading her way—troubles for which she would need, as before, Joe's special protection to survive. Closing her eyes, she repeated over and over: *Everything will be fine. Everything will be fine. Everything will be fine. Everything will be fine. Everything will be fine. Please let everything be fine.*

When Mara stepped off the ferry in Kodiak, she took all her things with her. Standing on the dock, she thought she saw a glimpse of Joe watching her from the upper deck, but whoever she saw was gone before she could really focus her eyes.

She walked slowly into town, bent over slightly under the burden of her bulging backpack. Her thick, long hair hung in a single braid down her back and her frayed wool sweater hung loosely over fleece pants that were tucked into her knee-high rubber boots. Her face was devoid of makeup, her nails no longer manicured and polished, and her skin tanned and lightly weathered from spending weeks out at sea. She was thinner now, making her seem taller. Few would have recognized her from the way she looked on her first days in Alaska slightly over a year ago.

She checked into a small hotel within walking distance of the harbor using a fake name. It probably didn't matter. She had never been to Kodiak before and even Doug's friends probably wouldn't recognize her as the same woman he had introduced them to in Homer only a few months earlier.

"Got a smoke?" a woman asked.

Mara looked up to see a woman about her own height, but a few years older, standing beside her.

"I don't smoke," she answered.

"Yeah. Sure. Figured," the woman said, squinting at Mara as she reached down the front of her blouse and pulled out a wad of bills. "Guess I'll have to tap into my savings."

"Sorry," Mara began before the woman thrust out her hand and said, "I'm Sally Kindle—Sal to my friends."

"I'm M—I'm Jane Brown," Mara said.

"It's a bitch, I know," Sal said, eyeing Mara up and down as she talked.

"What do you mean?" Mara replied.

"You know—finding somewhere to crash when your old man kicks you out, or yer lookin' for work, or whatever got you hangin' out on the streets with everything ya own on yer back like yer doin'."

"It's nothing like that," Mara said unconvincingly.

"Look, Jane—or whatever yer real name is—I got me a cabin in town. It ain't fancy, but it's clean enough and I got heat. Whatever yer runnin' from— well, you'll be safe there for now."

"I'll be heading out on the ferry in two days," Mara said in the way of explanation.

"Come on, Jane," Sal said, picking up Mara's pack. "Let's get you somewhere safe till then."

CHAPTER TWENTY TWO

Clam Chowder

SAL'S PLACE WAS A SHORT WALK FROM THE HARBOR AND ONE OF A ROW OF wooden cabins built on pilings along the water. Mara followed Sal down the boardwalk, noticing the pungent smell of the sea as they walked. The cabin had one window facing the boardwalk, but the far wall was largely glass, overlooking a small balcony that hung out over the water.

Inside the dimly lit cabin was a cramped but comfortable living space that held a sofa, a woodstove, a small table with two chairs, and a couple of large pillows on the floor—on one of which sat a tawny long-haired cat. Off to the side of the room was a small kitchen that housed a two-burner gas stove, a vintage refrigerator, and a double sink. A single bedroom could be seen off the living area. Mara presumed that space held a bathroom as well.

"Look, the bed's yours to use for a couple of days if ya want. Truth is, I could use the security and someone to feed my cat while I go out on my old man's boat to pick up some crab pots in the morning. I'll be back just about the time you say yer leavin'."

"But why are you doing this?" Mara asked her. "I mean, I could rob you blind for all you know."

"Look, Jane," Sal said, bringing over a kettle of hot water from the wood-stove and pouring some over the tea bags she had placed in two antique china cups on the table. "I been in yer shoes, okay?"

"But—" Mara tried to protest.

"Jane, I been there, okay? Ya don't need ta explain nothin' ta me, okay? I seen ya in town and I saw the same look I seen on twenty others like ya—lost—scared—runnin' from somethin' or someone—or maybe even from somethin' ya don't even know yet. Ya don't owe me no explanation and ya don't owe me nothin' but to watch over my place and maybe help someone else who needs it down the road. Now how 'bout some homemade clam chowder one of my neighbors brought down this mornin'?"

Mara liked Sal at once. Beneath her earthy façade, she saw a compassionate and caring person. She looked around at the small cabin. It was as comfortable as any fine establishment she had visited. Beneath the china cups and the china plates that did not match was an old wooden table with delicately spiraled legs and equally vintage chairs that also did not match. The table was covered in a white handmade lace table cover on which Sal had placed smaller versions in a rich blue that served as placemats. Each of the two chairs had seat pads made of floral cotton attached to the chair back by ribbons tied in neat bows. A candle burned inside a glass beaker on the table.

The two sat enjoying the chowder as darkness fell over the water. Sal even brought out a bottle of wine, which they shared while they talked about various moments in their lives. Mara said little about herself except that she had been married twice and was currently separated from her husband—adequate explanation, even if it was a slight distortion of the truth. Sal seemed to accept it, though, going on to talk about her own failed first marriage and her current arrangement with a man ten years older who kept asking her to marry him, but—as she told Mara—she just wasn't sure she wanted to risk it again.

"He's as good a man as they come," Sal said, "And one of these days I'm gonna put him outta his misery and say 'I do'. I just hope he don't keel over dead when I do," she laughed.

About midnight, Sal gathered up some of her things and showed Mara where the shower was, telling her she was going to sleep on the boat with her man, so they could leave at first light in the morning.

When Mara tried to thank her, Sal cut her off. "Just leave the key with old Doc down at the first cabin, and make sure the candle and the stove's out good. If ya get back here ever again, I hope ta see ya. Ya seem all right to me, Jane."

Mara impulsively hugged Sal, catching her off guard.

"Yup. Ya seem all right ta me," Sal repeated. "And, one last thing, Jane."

"What's that, Sal?" Mara said as she walked her to the door.

"Tell Joe thanks from me if ya see him again."

"Joe?" Mara asked.

"Joe Michael, Jane. He got me outta more'n one bind in my life and I wanna make sure someone tells him I'm okay."

With that shocking statement, Sal walked out, latching the door behind her and leaving Mara standing speechless in her newfound friend's cabin.

CHAPTER TWENTY THREE

Goodbye Kodiak

WHEN MARA WALKED UP TO THE END CABIN AT THE START OF THE BOARDWALK, she couldn't help but notice the old man sitting in a recliner inside. Smiling, she held up the keys and wiggled them, assuming he had been expecting that someone would be coming by to drop them off. He started to get up, but waved her in instead.

"Jest leave 'em on the table there—there'll be more after you," Doc said.

Seeing her puzzled expression, he added, "Sal's always bringin' by someone in need. Seems like strangers are there more'n she is anymore."

"Okay. Well, thank you," Mara answered, unsure of what else to say. "I'll be going now, and everything's locked up—the stove's out, and the candle— just like Sal asked me to leave it. Thanks, again. Bye now."

Clicking the door shut, she walked toward the ferry terminal, passing the hotel she had checked into before being taken in by Sal. Suddenly remembering that she still had the hotel key, she turned and walked back.

When she handed the key to the desk clerk, he went into a back room, returning with another man who said he was the proprietor. Mara recognized him from when she had registered.

"Didn't think I'd be see'n you again," he barked.

"I'm sorry I didn't bring the key earlier. I ended up staying with a friend," Mara answered.

"You gonna pay for the damages, or do I need to call the cops?" he demanded.

Turning to the clerk, he hissed, "Get Denton or one of his deputies over here."

"Damages?" Mara said.

"Typical," the obviously angry owner shot back. "None of ya drunks and crackheads ever remember all the mayhem once yer buzz wears off, do ya?"

"I beg your pardon," Mara said indignantly. "I'm neither a drunk, nor am I a crackhead, and as I already explained, I didn't occupy your room that night—and I did pay you in advance for the lease of the space."

"How ya gonna explain that door, then?" he said, squinting at her over his glasses.

"I don't know anything about a door," she replied tersely.

Mara knew she looked rumpled and thin, but how else could she look after having spent the last three weeks traveling on seiners and ferries in the remote waters of Alaska? No matter if she was not at her best right now, she was not about to be talked to like she was some kind of yesterday's trash.

"As if it is any of your business, I stayed with a woman named Sal Kindle over near the harbor, and the old man they call Doc can verify that if you choose not to believe me."

Mara's anger had risen as she spoke, creating an odd emotion as it mixed with the fear and aloneness she felt right now.

"Well, I did see Sal in town right about the time you checked in here," the proprietor said. "Seems she's always takin' in strays like you."

Indignation replaced Mara's fear.

"If, sir, you feel it is necessary to continue to take that tone with me, then it's a good thing your worker, here, has already called the cops, because I have no intention of standing here one minute longer and listening to any more of your baseless and downright insulting accusations."

The proprietor peered over his glasses and let his eyes bore into her for what seemed like a full minute. Finally, he told his clerk, "Tell Denton we ain't gonna need him or his men."

"I apologize, Miss," he said to Mara. "We've been havin' our share of trouble around here and when I found the door to your room kicked in and everything ransacked inside, I figured you was part of the problem. If you was with Sal, though, then that's good enough fer me."

Just then the door opened and Mara saw Sal walk in.

"You messin' with my cousin Jane, here, Pete?"

"Not messin' with anyone, Sal—yer cousin? Gol, Sal—If yer willin' ta vouch fer her, then I guess I—"

"I'm willin' Pete," Sal interrupted him. "Find yerself another tree to bark up, 'cause cousin' Jane's been house-sittin' fer me for the last two days."

"Thank you," Mara whispered to Sal.

Turning to Pete, she said, "Although, as I told you, I have no idea of who kicked in the door to my room, I do feel some sense of responsibility for inconveniencing you by leaving it unattended when you thought it was occupied. Would a hundred dollars plus one night's rent seem fair compensation to you?" Reaching into her pocket, she passed a hundred-dollar bill across the counter.

"I'll consider it resolved," Pete said, pocketing the bill. "Didn't think you looked the type to run with a bunch of Mexican punks anyway."

"Mexicans?" Mara asked, raising one eyebrow, as she looked him straight in the eye.

"I'm guessin' they was Mexicans. Looked like Mexicans. Talked like Mexicans—ya know, talkin' Spanish with a few words of broken English mixed in now and then. We get a lot of 'em up here lookin' fer work on the boats."

"Well, that is all news to me, just as whoever they might be is also news to me," Mara responded.

Without saying any more to him, she turned and walked out the door, stopping to thank Sal one more time, and reminding her that she had left the key with Doc and closed up the cabin just as instructed.

"I know you're headin' to Seward next," Sal said, catching Mara by surprise. "Don't look so shocked. When ya live down here, ya know all the ferry's comin's and goin's.

"All I'm sayin', Jane, is I want ya ta stay safe. Anyone asks, I ain't seen anyone I don't know around here in weeks—except for my cousin, Jane, who went back home to Peoria after visitin' fer a couple of days. Ya take care now, okay?"

Mara watched Sal walk away. When she boarded the ferry, she flashed the special pass with her photo and an ID code underneath, and walked to her stateroom locking the door behind her. As the *Kennicott* pulled away from Kodiak, she watched the fuzzy forms of people moving around down on the docks through the scratchy window on the far wall of her stateroom.

When she got to Seward, she would use a pay phone and a calling card to phone Doug. Instinctively she knew that using her cell phone was now too risky.

CHAPTER TWENTY FOUR

Home

DOUG WAITED UNTIL THE LAST CAR HAD UNLOADED TO GET OFF THE FERRY, pretending that he was a passenger waiting for one of the trucks. When he walked along the wide dock leading to the Homer ferry terminal, the sun was setting behind the mountains of the Alaska Range, directly across Cook Inlet. It was unusual to see the tall peaks across the water, and when they appeared it usually meant the day had been sunny and clear.

He watched the sun sink behind the mountains, leaving the sky a brilliant glow of color that reminded him of the orange popsicles he had enjoyed as a child. The mountains, at first colored in the soft pink of alpenglow, soon became dark silhouettes against the sky. Above him, hundreds of circling gulls squawked over the beaches before they fell silent, as day became night.

Except for a semi truck that was jockeying into position to unload the trailer sent over with the rest of the cargo, most of the vehicles onboard the ferry had been unloaded and were being driven by their owners up the Spit road toward town. Doug watched the truck for a few minutes, amazed that such a large vehicle could be squeezed onto the turnstile that lowered the vehicles to the car deck of the ferry. After a while, he retied an old blue bandana around his head, slung his pack over his shoulder and hitched a ride with a tourist from Anchorage to the top of Baycrest Hill.

From there he backtracked about a mile before turning down a side road that led to his and Mara's house. She had purchased it on first arriving in Homer, and marriage to him had not dampened her desire to stay there. Doug liked the house, too. The view of the sea was expansive and he could see the boats coming and going to their fishing grounds. He supposed they would stay there forever—if they could get through whatever danger they were in and actually have a future.

The place looked undisturbed, which gave him the only reassurance he had felt since leaving for Sitka. He noticed that the answering machine was full, and did not bother to check who was calling. He knew it would be Ellie and maybe even Ben Donaley. Perhaps the investigators were even trying to reach him by now. No matter, anyway; it wasn't going to change a thing if he listened.

He took a shower and put on a fresh change of clothes. It felt good to be home, clean in his own shower. The refrigerator smelled of rotting food, most of which he swept into a garbage bag, which he then lowered into another for extra protection. He gave the refrigerator shelves a quick wipe-down, drank some of the juice that still looked good, and fell onto the bed for a couple of hours' sleep, not even bothering to pull down the covers.

Before sunrise, he packed a couple of changes of clothes into a canvas bag, throwing his .44 on top just in case, and walked through the kitchen into the garage. It was 4 a.m. when he backed his truck out of the garage and pushed the remote to close the door. He watched it close gently as he pulled away. If anyone saw him, he wasn't concerned. The neighbors were used to long absences and early-morning departures. He doubted if anyone had even been aware that he had been home. He hadn't bothered to tell anyone he was back or that he felt his boat had been sabotaged. Right now the stakes couldn't be higher and he just wanted to get his bearings again.

On the way out of town he stopped at a dumpster and dropped in the garbage bag filled with the spoiled food from the refrigerator. Driving off, he lowered both windows of his truck to air out the inside, cussing at himself for not having thrown the rancid mess into the truck bed instead of the cab. By 6 a.m. he was pulling out of Soldotna, having stopped there briefly for a cup of coffee and a breakfast sandwich, which he ate as he drove.

He had already passed the silhouettes of at least eleven browsing moose—reminding him to take it slow for the next hour or so as they began to move across their range. He stopped again in Cooper Landing, this time for more coffee and a couple of donuts, before heading past Tern Lake and taking the cutoff left to Anchorage.

Turnagain Pass was ablaze in the morning sun. It looked like another clear day was coming. Blinded by the sunlight against the glaring white of the snow-covered mountains, he fumbled for his sunglasses in the glove box—finally locating them and slipping them onto his face. Man, they were filthy! After several attempts to wipe them with the edge of his shirt, he pulled into a turnout and cleaned them with some leftover bottled water he had left in the cup holder in the door. Much better.

When he looked up, he saw a pack of wolves walking single file along the far side of the still frozen Summit Lake. He sat there watching them, enjoying the rare treat in spite of his need to get to Palmer as soon as possible. Perhaps seeing them was a sign—an omen of good fortune ahead. He could use some good fortune about now. He was getting tired of living on the run. He took out his wallet and pulled out a picture of Mara that he kept tucked in the back. Could she feel him thinking about her, loving her from who knew how many miles away now?

He looked at the wolves again, knowing that it was only wishful thinking that good fortune lie ahead. Despite his deep love for his own wolf dog, Thor, experience had taught him that seeing a wild wolf pack was seldom a good omen.

CHAPTER TWENTY-FIVE

Fatherly Love

BEN DONALEY STEPPED DOWN OFF THE TRACTOR HE HAD BEEN USING TO grade Ellie's driveway.

"Wasn't sure how you two made out," he told Doug. "I heard about the seiner. Knew you were safe and all. Is Mara—"

"She's safe," Doug answered, not letting Ben finish asking the question foremost on his mind. "I expect someone's going to wanna be talkin' to me about the seiner."

"Our agency has already been in touch with the Coast Guard and they have been made officially aware that neither you nor Mara were involved with the demise of the *Roamer*," Ben said. "Still, they're probably going to want to talk to you to verify that, especially since two crew members were on board and suffered some effects from the cold water immersion—not to mention being thrown off the vessel by the blast."

Ben saw Doug tense up at the mention of the two crew members and added, "Luckily they're both okay and, aside from some bruises and a night or two in the hospital for observation, there are no other issues with them— except with my agency wanting to know just how much they saw or knew about the tampering with your seiner."

"Ellie inside?" Doug asked, brushing past Ben.

He was tired and he missed Mara. It had taken him nearly forty years to find her and now, due to some wild and confusing circumstances, they were apart. Wasn't it enough that his only brother had been murdered, or that his longtime girlfriend had somehow been involved and that she, too, was now murdered?

Falling in love with Mara had been the only bright spot in his recent past. He prayed she was okay. She had a good head on her shoulders. She had proven that when managing the seiner in the middle of the herring fishery while he lay in the hospital recovering from emergency surgery.

Instinct told him to not try to call her from Palmer, not even using a pay phone. He would visit with Ellie, and his young niece, Anna, and maybe he would check on Sarah and Ken, before heading back out to let the latest drama in his life play out.

Ben Donaley's voice brought Doug back to the present. "Ellie and Anna are staying with Sarah and Ken for a while. Ellie took Anna up there the minute they heard about the seiner. She tried to come home for a bit, but after she had been here for close to a week, I convinced her to go back up there for Anna's safety, not to mention for her own."

"That's good," Doug replied. "Especially since I can't be around to keep an eye on them. All that's happened here…can't even bear to think about…"

Doug's voice trailed off as he remembered the shooting that had left Mara's husband dead, Sassy's brother killed by her own hand, and his own dog, Thor, injured right here in this very yard.

Ben struggled to control the emotion he felt at the thought of the tragedy this young family had endured. Why was he having so much trouble maintaining the neutral distance that had always served him so well while performing his job with the IPA?

He hadn't been the same, really, since his only son had been gunned down right here in the yard where he now stood. Maybe it was time to retire. He wanted to tell Doug all of that, perhaps even take him under his wing in the way he had taken care of his own son. He found it strange and ironic that Doug had touched a chord in him, and even stranger that Doug had fallen in love with and married Brad's young widow.

Instead, he swallowed hard and climbed back up onto the tractor and fired it up.

"You go on up and check on 'em all," he told Doug. "It'll make you feel a bit better. I'll be keeping watch down this way along with a couple of agents from the FBI that Ellie has been letting stay in the bunkhouse until you got back—speaking of which, are you gonna need to stay there?"

"I'll stay up with the others for tonight and part of tomorrow and then I'll head out again. I'll probably stop in and talk to the Coast Guard—though I'll be danged if I know how I'm gonna explain Mara not bein' with me," Doug answered.

"Don't worry about what they think," Ben said. "Once their report gets sent up to the FBI, agents there will know how to handle it. Meanwhile, just tell them she had to go Outside for a family emergency or something you think they will believe, and concentrate on keeping the both of you safe."

Reaching up to Ben, Doug extended his hand in gratitude. "'preciate it, Ben…'preciate all you're doin' to watch our backs."

The sound of the tractor revving up muffled Ben's emotional, "No problem, son." Just as the smoke from the stack made the tears in Ben's eyes seem like nothing more than a reaction to the thick, black cloud generated by the tractor.

Ten minutes later Doug was pulling into the driveway of the home of Ken and Sarah Tandry. Ben Donaley seemed like a decent guy. He hoped his instinct about the man was right. Lately, nothing he trusted had stayed either normal or predictable.

CHAPTER TWENTY-SIX

Time for Caution

ANNA WAS STANDING IN THE FRONT DOORWAY ON THE SECOND STORY, which housed the living quarters in Ken and Sarah's house. Just outside a wooden fence that formed a courtyard at the foot of the stairs, a full-grown moose reached its head over the landing and watched her.

Doug could see Thor poking his head out the door beside Anna. Just as he had taught him, Thor did not bark at the moose.

"Sh-h-h," Anna signaled to Doug by holding one finger up over pursed lips.

Knowing she was reasonably safe, Doug sat in his truck and watched her as she and the moose maintained eye contact.

"I'm sorry I can't give you any food. It's a'legal," he heard her say. "I know you're hungry and I know it's cold out there, but you have a nice fur coat and you will just have to wait outside and look for some food. I'm going in now."

Anna started to shut the door and then opened it up, leaning out as she spoke, "Don't try to follow me, now. You're too big to come inside. Bye."

Doug watched the six-year-old shut the door. Moments later the moose turned and wandered off. Before he could even step all the way out of his truck, Anna came bounding out the lower-level garage door.

"Uncle Dougy! Uncle Dougy! Uncle Dougy!" Throwing her arms around his neck as he stooped to pick her up. "Momm-ee-ee! It's Uncle Dougy," she screamed over her shoulder. "Hurry!"

"You're not glad to see me, now are you, Anna?" Doug teased, as he set her on her feet on the ground while Thor nuzzled up to him demanding equal attention. "How you doin', buddy?"

"Where's Aunt Mara?" Anna said, suddenly serious.

"Yes, where is Mara?" Ellie said as she walked out the garage door and hugged Doug. "We've all been worried sick about you two."

"I know. I'm sorry," Doug fumbled. "Ben Donaley told me you were up here."

"Ben's been a godsend for us," Ellie said. "But where's Mara? Is she okay? Are the two of you okay?"

"Mara's fine," Doug directed his answer to both Ellie and her daughter.

Leaning down to pet Thor he said, "Anna, why don't you run upstairs and see if you can get me something cold to drink."

"Okay, Uncle Doug," Anna laughed as she skipped off toward the house. "We got soda. We got water in bottles. We got milk. We got juice…"

"Juice will taste fine, Anna. Now hurry, I'm really thirsty after the long drive."

Now that they were alone, Doug's voice took on a more serious tone. "Mara's safe, Ellie. I'm not telling anyone where she is, but trust me that she is safe. She's planning to call you and Sarah tonight or tomorrow to let you know that."

"But why can't you tell us where she is, Doug? Why isn't she with you? What happened with the seiner?"

"Ellie," Doug answered, pausing to choose his words carefully. "When Dan died…when Sassy shot A.C.…even when Mara's missing husband turned up under an assumed name…when all that happened, I thought nothing that bad could ever happen to any of us again."

Ellie furrowed her brow as she listened, stopping to take a bottle of juice from Anna who had run down from the kitchen with it. "You go stay with Aunt Sarah now, Anna."

"Okay, Mommy."

Once Anna was out of hearing range, Doug continued, "The sense of relief that it was all finally over, then, was greater than I ever imagined. When Mara and I got married, both of us said the same thing—that we thought we could never have imagined being this happy. Somehow we decided that our marriage was the only good thing that had come out of something so bad—that and Sarah meeting and marrying Ken, and the fact that you and Anna were safe."

"Where are you going with this, Doug?" Ellie insisted. "Something's wrong. You tell me, Doug Williams!"

By now Ellie was shaking. She had been through too much to not pick up on the unease emanating from her normally calm brother-in-law.

"Are you sure Mara is safe? What's going on, Doug?"

"Ellie, calm down," Doug said. "Calm down or I won't tell you any more. I don't want you letting even a hint of my concern show to Sarah or to Anna."

"Okay, Doug. I'm sorry. It's just that I can see you're upset. You're a good man—just like Dan was. It's just that I can't bear thinking that there could be any more to this nightmare we've been living."

Doug waited a few minutes as Ellie composed herself before continuing.

"I have reason to believe that the tampering with my seiner and its explosion at sea were no coincidence," he told her.

"Oh, Doug…" Ellie put her hand over her mouth to try to keep her exclamation muffled.

"I'm not sure what's going on, Ellie, but there are a couple more things I just can't tell you about right now. I'm asking you to trust me. I'm your husband's only brother and the godfather to your only daughter. Trust me, Ellie, when I tell you that your safety, Mara's safety—all our safety is the only thing that matters to me."

"You're scaring me," Ellie whispered.

"I'm a little scared myself, Ellie," Doug answered. "I want you to stay up here with Ken and Sarah—maybe consider sending Anna to stay with one of her friends for a while again, just like you did before when none of us knew what was going on with Dan's plane crash."

"But the homestead…"

"Ben Donaley will take good care of things there, Ellie. And don't forget that Ken has a couple of federal agents up there in the bunkhouse."

"But where will you stay?" Ellie asked.

"I'm heading back to Homer in the morning," he answered. "Please trust me, Ellie. Do as I ask."

Just then Anna came running out into the yard again. "Mommy! Uncle Doug! It's Aunt Mara on the phone."

CHAPTER TWENTY-SEVEN

Phone Call

BOTH ELLIE AND DOUG SPRINTED UP THE STAIRS TO THE LIVING ROOM where they found Sarah talking tearfully on the phone.

"I'm sorry, Mara. It's just that I'm so worried about you, and this pregnancy has left my emotions all over the place. Here, you talk to Ellie and your husband—I know—I love you, too."

Sarah held onto her huge belly with her left hand and handed the phone to Ellie with her right.

"Please, Anna, would you go get Aunt Sarah a cold washcloth? I just want to lay my head back for a few minutes while Mommy and Uncle Doug talk to Aunt Mara."

For the next ten minutes, Ellie talked to Mara, filling her in on all the happenings with Sarah and her pregnancy, the details about the nursery that Ken and she had put together under Sarah's supervision, and how she had taught Anna to knit so she could try to make baby booties for her new cousin.

Ellie told her about how she was making a custom fleece baby blanket with the baby's name appliquéd in satin letters down one side.

"No, I can't tell you the name or the baby's sex," Ellie said with false indignation. "I've been sworn to secrecy on both. No, Mara," she laughed, "I can't and I won't tell you what color the blanket is!"

By the time Doug picked up the phone, Mara was fully homesick for her Alaska family and told her husband so in her own tearful moment. Wanting to talk to his wife privately, Doug took the phone with him down to his truck and sat inside.

He found it hard to keep his voice steady as he assured Mara that the day-to-day things in their lives were okay. He told her about cleaning out the refrigerator, remembering to set the alarm on the house when he left, how Ben Donaley had reassured him about the investigation and had convinced Ellie and Anna to move up to Ken and Sarah's place, and he even relayed the conversation he had just had with Ellie about possibly sending Anna to live with a friend's family for a few weeks—just in case.

He asked if she was safe? Had she seen any more of Joe Michael and did she have enough money to get by? He commended her on having the good sense to use a disposable phone and calling card to contact him, and listened intently as she told him about Sal Kindle's strange words when she had left Kodiak.

"I can't explain it, Doug," she told her husband, "but I feel safe out here— as though some invisible force is watching over me."

He guessed that was some reassurance. He wasn't sure why.

"Ellie knows we could be in danger," he told Mara. "Although she'll never know it, I'm going to ask Ben to hook her phone up to a secure line that she can access from Sarah's. That way, Ben can monitor any strange calls that might come into the house and he can also transfer my calls to Ellie without anyone but him knowing it's me.

"Yes, I know it's a risk," he said, "but I don't think Ben is going to work against us, and we have no choice but to trust somebody. As far as Ellie is concerned, she will believe that she is the only link to me, and I trust her to keep that between us."

Mara kissed the wedding ring Doug had placed on her finger as he told her he loved her. By the time the recorded message announced that there were 59 seconds left on the card, they both fell silent, until a sudden click kept either of them from having to say goodbye.

A good half hour later, Doug was still sitting in his truck wondering how life could have taken such a cruel turn. He pounded his fist angrily into the console before realizing that Anna was standing outside his truck.

"I miss Aunt Mara, too," Anna said after opening the door and climbing up on the running board to try to pull him out of the driver's seat. "Thor wants you to come inside now," and Doug Williams did just as his young niece told him to.

CHAPTER TWENTY-EIGHT

Fire...Again

As Doug drove the Old Glenn Highway toward Palmer the next day, several emergency vehicles with sirens screamed past him. Off to the right, a column of black smoke roared into the air before drifting into in a thin, hazy line that moved with the wind along the mountains.

The smoke looked suspiciously close to Sassy's place. Turning down the side road he had driven so many times back when he and Sassy were a couple, he reached the driveway behind the first fire engine, where he could see Sassy's hired hand, Stan, running the horses out of the burning barn.

When he jumped out of his truck to try to help Stan, an emergency worker who told him to stay back stopped him. Pushing past him, he ran toward Stan and helped lead the horses to the far pasture, well away from the barn.

"Thanks, Doug. That was the last one," an exhausted Stan gasped.

The entire structure was an inferno as first the roof, and then the walls of the barn caved in.

"This don't surprise me at all," Stan repeated over and over, his voice raspy and an audible wheeze squeaking with each breath. "Knew somethin' like this would happen. Just knew it."

"What're you sayin', Stan?" Doug asked him. "Here. Sit down and rest before you fall down. Just sit still now, and catch your breath."

"I mean strange things have been goin' on around here, startin' with the danged-awful murder of Amanda Carlson," Stan spat out. "What the blazes you doin' here, anyway, Doug? I heard you got married and were fishing somewhere out around Sitka anymore."

"I did get married, Stan," Doug told him. "Not sure if you ever met her. We were fishing out near Sitka, but we ran into some strange situations ourselves, and so I came back to check on…Well, it's a long story. Anyway, we live in Homer now, Mara and me. So, I guess whoever's managing Sassy's estate kept you around to look after things, huh?" Doug said, changing the subject.

"Estate's been settled for several weeks," Stan answered, spitting the sentence out in spurts as if the struggle to breathe was his normal. "I'm here workin' for Erin, now."

"Erin?" Doug asked, not recognizing the name.

"Sassy's daughter. Her name's Erin," Stan answered.

"Sassy didn't have a daughter. I would have known that."

"Seems you didn't, Williams. Seems no one did. But, sure enough, Miss Amanda Carlson had a daughter that she gave away at birth. I know it's true. I've seen all the paperwork—talked to the lawyers when the estate settled— the whole ball of wax."

Doug removed and reseated his hat on his head. "How old is she?"

"About twenty-two," Stan answered, not letting all his wheezing keep him from telling Doug the news.

"Seems that Sassy got pregnant at a young age—about fifteen—raped. The story I heard was that she and A.C. was homeless at the time and so she signed the baby over to this rich couple in California. Erin showed up here about two years ago—said the mother that raised her knew all about it—even gave it her blessing, I guess."

Stan stopped talking for a moment while he gasped for more air. Pulling a wrinkled bandana out of his pocket, he blew his nose before continuing.

"She's been sending Miz Carlson money on a regular basis ever since. I know this for a fact, because Miz Carlson told me about it more'n once. She was pretty happy that her daughter found her like she did. Told me it helped make up for the pain of having given her away way back when. Said it wasn't the money that made her happy, it was jest knowin' that her daughter turned out okay and didn't hate her for givin' her up. She was like that, Miz Carlson, more carin' than most folks knew."

Doug listened to Stan tell him all the details he knew about Sassy's daughter, Erin. In all the years he and Sassy had been together, she had never mentioned either a rape or a child. How could she have ever kept such a secret? Apparently there was a lot about his former lover that he had never known.

It surprised him that with each new layer that peeled off Sassy's brassy persona, a more gentle and tender side to Amanda Carlson emerged.

Mara had seen that side of Sassy and had often encouraged him to give her a second chance. Sadly, he would never be able to tell Sassy that he now knew many of the secrets of her past—secrets that revealed a woman of stronger character and higher moral standards than he or anyone else had ever given her credit for while she was alive.

He closed his eyes and said a silent prayer that Sassy's soul had found its way to heaven. If it had, he prayed, could she please forgive him for the indifference and sometimes harshness he had shown her.

"I wish I had known this when she was still alive," Doug told Stan. "I just wish I would have known. Now, let's get you inside and rested up a bit."

"Yeah. I could use a cigarette," Stan answered.

CHAPTER TWENTY-NINE

Doug Meets Erin

DOUG COULD HARDLY BELIEVE WHAT HE WAS SEEING. TALL AND THIN, WITH long blond hair filled with pink highlights falling past her shoulders, Erin De la Corte was the mirror image of a younger Amanda Carlson. He watched her step out of the car being driven by a young man about her same age. Her resemblance to Sassy was unmistakable.

Stan pushed past him and rushed to her, but not before she could react to the sight of the burned-out barn.

"What happened here, Stan? Are you all right? I can't believe this. First my mother is murdered, then my father is beaten, and now this."

"The horses are all safe, Miss De la Corte. That's all that matters. The barn can be re-built."

Erin was visibly distraught. "Stan, are you okay? You're wheezing! Carlos has cursed me."

"Calm down, Erin," the young man sitting beside her said before turning to Doug. "I'm Ethan Shepherd, and you are?"

"Doug Williams," Doug answered. "I was a close friend of Amanda Carlson, the former owner of this ranch."

"You knew my mother?" Erin said, suddenly more interested in this stranger than in what had just happened to her barn.

"I knew her well," Doug answered. "She and I were involved with each other for about three years. She never mentioned she had a daughter, though."

"I'm Erin De la Corte," the young woman said, extending her hand in greeting. "Amanda Carlson was my birth mother, but we only found each other two years ago. The mother and father who raised me live in California."

"I'm Doug Williams," Doug repeated, extending his hand to the young woman. "I'm sorry about your mother. We weren't together any more when she died," he said, "but it was a tragedy to lose her like we did, just the same."

"Oh, you're that Doug Williams, "she blurted out.

Doug raised his eyebrows but otherwise did not react.

"I don't know what you heard about me or who you heard it from…"

"I heard plenty and I heard it straight from my mother," Erin snapped.

"I'm not sure what your mother told you then," Doug said evenly, "but if it's anything other than that I did my best to be straight with her, then I can't do anymore than tell you that our relationship had its ups and it had its downs and that eventually we broke up. She knew the truth and so did I and the rest doesn't matter."

"Whatever…" Erin said, reaching back to get her things out of the car. "It's not my business."

"Look, Erin, I'm sorry you may have heard some things that upset you.

"It's more than likely you're going to hear more stories around town about your mother. There's an even better chance that most of 'em will be true. But, whatever you hear, always remember one thing. Although your mother had her fair share of troubles and had a reputation that far outweighed anything that could have really happened, she was a decent person."

"Decent person, you say? Not decent enough for you two to stay together, apparently," Erin snapped, surprised at her own temerity.

Doug forced his voice to stay even, "I'm not sure I deserved that, Miss De la Corte. Like I said, I'm not sure what you may have heard about me and your mother—"

"Just that you wouldn't marry her," Erin shot back. "That's all she wanted, you know, was for you to marry her."

"I know she said she wanted that—Erin, did you say your name was? The truth, though, is that your mother loved another man more than she loved me. In the end, she lost us both."

"Then I apologize to you, Mr. Williams," Erin said, regaining her composure. "I have no idea why I said what I did. You are a total stranger to me. Until now, I had never even met you. All I know is your name and what my mother told me. I'm just upset about the fire and some other things. Please forgive my rudeness. Of all people, I should be the last to judge you."

"No need to apologize, Miss De la Corte…"

"Please, I hope you will call me Erin."

"I accept your apology for words spoken by a young woman who has suddenly lost the mother she never knew," Doug continued. "I'm sorry you lost her just when you were finding her."

"Thank you Mr. Williams. You seem like a decent person."

"Please call me Doug," he replied.

"I live in Homer with my wife, Mara. I just happened to be visiting my sister-in-law, Ellie Williams, up on Knik River Road." Doug said pointing toward the Knik Glacier, "and saw the smoke as I drove into town. I know this place so well. Lucky it was only the barn and not the house—and that all the animals and Stan are safe."

"Thank you for stopping and for helping," Erin said.

"I met Ellie Williams. She brought me some things that belonged to my mother. You're her brother-in-law? And you were close to my mother? I wonder—if you have time—before you go—would you consider—could you possibly tell me more about my mother?"

"It would be my great pleasure to do that," Doug answered. "But first let me help you, Stan, and Ethan tend to the horses."

"The barn," she said, as though suddenly realizing her loss. "There's nothing left."

CHAPTER THIRTY

Meltdown

"CORDOVA'S A GOOD PLACE TO SPEND A COUPLA DAYS," JOE MICHAEL SAID as he stood next to Mara on the deck of the Alaska ferry *Aurora*.

"It's you," Mara told him. "Always turning up when I least expect it."

"It's what I do," he answered simply. "Hey, look. See that black bear over on the shore?"

Mara looked at the old man and shrugged disinterestedly, not even bothering to speak.

"Better toughen up," Joe Michael told her. "It ain't over yet."

Mara tried to ignore him. She was tired of the disarray that had become her life.

"I see you're in a bad mood," he said, walking away.

Still she did not respond.

Joe Michael stopped to watch her for a minute before walking back her way. Reaching into his pocket, he pulled out a feather and handed it to her. "Better take this back. It's starting to look kinda ratty, but it still works."

Suddenly Mara whirled around, her eyes blazing with all the anger she held inside at the sequence of bad luck—no, not bad *luck,* more like bad karma—that had followed her the last five years.

"Why are you following me? I mean, really, Why? Don't you have other people to go help? I don't want this stupid feather. Last time you gave me the flippin' feather, three people died. Even you died—but, not really. I hate this feather. It means nothing but heartache and uncertainty to me."

That said, she impulsively threw the feather overboard and watched it whirl slowly downward, before a gust of wind blew it upward, where it landed it gently at her feet.

"Look, I understand your fear," Joe said, picking the feather up and smoothing its edges—pausing with his fingers at the red dot painted on the long edge. "But this is no time to lose it. You have a husband to think of, too."

Mara stared at him and at the feather he held between his thumb and forefinger before reaching out and taking it from his hand.

"I'm sorry," she said simply, as she put the feather in her pocket.

"Sal said you were looking a little rough in Kodiak," Joe continued.

"That's another thing," Mara shot back. "What's with Sal? I mean, she's a good person and all that, but do you have some kind of cult thing going on out there or what?"

"Not if you call findin' the new love of my life a cult," Joe answered.

"You? Sal?" Mara gasped.

Just then she remembered how Sal had told her she was meeting up with her "old man" on his crab boat.

"You're Sal's crab fisherman?" Mara said, still stunned.

"I know. I can hardly believe it myself," Joe said. "Who'd a thought an old geezer like me could hook up with a dish like Sal, huh?"

"But she told me to tell you she was okay when I left Kodiak," Mara told him.

"That was just to throw you off track," Joe chuckled. "That's one thing I love about her."

"But she said you wanted her to marry you and she said no."

"Well, that's true enough," Joe answered. "But I got nothin' but time and a woman like Sal's worth the wait."

Mara was somewhere between surprise and disbelief at Joe's words. Could life get any stranger?

"Look," Joe persisted. "Hold onto the feather like I told you. Worked last time, didn't it?"

"Okay," Mara answered. "I can't explain why, but I trust you."

Breaking into a smile, she added, "And in spite of trying not to, I even kinda like you, too."

"What's not to like?" Joe asked wryly, winking at Mara. "I'm old but I still got it, you know."

CHAPTER THIRTY-ONE

Phone Call

WHEN MARA CALLED DOUG FROM THE PAY PHONE IN CORDOVA, BEN Donaley, as he had promised, intercepted and scrambled her call to all but Doug's
phone. It was a security measure that Doug appreciated more and more the
longer he and Mara were apart. At least, on some level, whoever or whatever
was interfering with their lives would not be able to use their precious conversations together to find them.

"You'll never believe what's been happening here," Doug told her.

"Really? It's getting kind of weird here, too," Mara answered.

""How are you holding up?" Doug asked his wife.

"I can't stand us being apart like this," she told him. "After Brad disappeared, I never thought I would love anyone again. Now, just when I do,
something bigger than both of us is coming between us. I just don't get it and
I definitely don't like it."

Mara paused, but the long silence felt more to Doug like a distant embrace
than any kind of awkward break in the conversation. "I love you and I miss
you," she whispered.

"I love you more," he answered, half laughing. He knew he dared not
get serious or he would not be able to keep Mara strong. "It'll be over soon.
Nothing lasts forever."

"Don't say that. Take it back!" Mara answered.

"You know what I mean," Doug said.

"Take it back, Doug."

"I take it back," he replied. "You know I was just trying to make you feel better."

"I know," Mara answered. "But we have enough going against us without hexing ourselves."

"I stopped at Ellie's after leaving Homer, and Ben Donaley told me she had taken Anna and Thor and gone up to stay with Sarah," Doug said, trying not to let Mara pick up on the uncertainty he felt. "When I went up there, Ellie grilled me pretty good, so I told her my suspicions about the boat, that she could and should trust Ben Donaley, and that you would be calling soon. Right after that you called."

"It was so good to talk to her and Sarah again," Mara answered. "How did Sarah look?"

"Big as a barn, and maybe a little pale," he answered. "Ken said he's pretty worried—something about anemia and strong vitamins the doctor's making her take now."

"Hearing about Sarah makes me sad about us not being able to have children," Mara said. "And I imagine it does you, too. It makes me feel I cheated you."

"Mara. Stop it!" Doug said. "I didn't marry you because you could or could not have children. I married you because I love you. I felt then and I feel now that if children come our way somehow, it will just be a stronger extension of our love—but if they don't, I'm okay with that, too. It's you I love, you and all the pieces and parts that are you. Besides, we'll have our hands full spoiling Anna and the new baby."

"Are you sure you haven't changed your mind about that and about marrying me?" Mara asked him.

"If I were there, I'd..." he told her.

"I know," she answered. "I just miss you and don't want you to forget about me."

"Mara!" Doug chastised her. "Let's stop tormenting ourselves and talk about your news."

"I talked with Joe Michael again," she said.

"Where?" Doug asked.

"On the ferry," she answered.

"Anything important?" Doug asked, knowing that no conversation with the Native elder was unimportant.

"He knows someone I met in Kodiak—a woman who took me in," Mara replied. "Her name is Sal."

Mara then proceeded to tell Doug the story of how Sal had taken her in and had rescued her when she went back to return her key to the hotel. When she finished, she told him about the words Sal had spoken about saying hi to Joe Michael.

"When Joe and I talked on the ferry yesterday, he told me about a new woman in his life. Unbelievably, it turns out she's Sal. Kinda makes her knowing about me make a little more sense now. Seems that Joe has a thing for Sal, and that Sal has a thing for old Joe," she told Doug.

"Wow. Who would have guessed that something like this would come up," he answered.

"The most important thing, though, was that he gave me the feather again," Mara said.

"The same feather?"

"Yes, the same feather. I got angry and threw it overboard," she told her husband.

"Mara!"

"But it got caught by the wind and blew upward, landing at my feet again," she explained.

Mara reached into her pocket. Feeling the feather there was unsettling in the same way it had been the first time Joe had given it to her on her way up to Alaska.

"What do you think it means?" Doug asked her.

"I don't know. I'm frightened. Joe said not to panic. He said I had you to think of, too. He said it wasn't over yet, and when I told him I was sick of the feather, he told me to hang onto it. 'It worked before,' he told me."

The feather had "worked before." Over and over its appearance had marked the onset of trouble and her escape from harm. How could she have been angry at him for giving it to her again—except in knowing that her troubles were not yet over.

"Do you have it now?" Doug asked her.

"Yes," she replied.

"Then do as Joe says, Mara."

"I will," she answered.

Doug hesitated to tell her the rest of his news.

"It looks like I'm going to be here a couple of more days," he began.

"I know you said you could be a few days. What else is going on?" she asked.

"Yesterday on my way into Palmer, I saw smoke in the Butte—right about at Sassy's place. Sure enough, when I got there the barn was fully engulfed in flames. I helped Stan get the horses to safety and then we sat and talked for a while."

"Any idea of how the barn caught fire?" Mara asked.

"No idea," Doug answered. "But there's more."

"More?" she asked.

"It seems that Sassy had a daughter?"

"A daughter? How could we not have known about that?" Mara asked him. "Are you sure she is really Sassy's daughter?"

"No one knew, far as I can tell," Doug answered. "Her name's Erin De la something, and Stan says she's about twenty-two. He checked out her story and apparently he was involved in the closing of Sassy's estate. He said Sassy left a simple will and left everything to her daughter and about twenty thousand dollars to Stan because of his loyalty to her."

"Wow!" Mara gasped.

"I met Erin. She was a bit hostile at first, but then explained how she only found her birth mother two years ago—that would be Sassy—something about Sassy being raped at fifteen and giving the baby up for adoption. She said she had heard about me from her mother. During our conversation, she said she guessed there were probably two sides to the story and so she was sorry she had been rude."

"Poor Sassy. Raped. Having a child at fifteen. Wow! How can you not feel for her and all the pain she went through? Why do some people have to suffer so much?" Mara said.

"I knew you would see it that way," Doug said, smiling through the phone. "It's just one of the reasons I love you."

"You know as well as anyone that I'm far from perfect, Doug Williams," Mara playfully admonished him.

"One of the reasons I want to stick around is that Erin asked me to tell her about her mother. I think for the sake of Sassy's legacy with her daughter—especially since they had just recently found each other and seemed to be on very good terms—that Erin hear about her from me before she hears all the scuttlebutt on the streets. Most of it is little more than embellishment and gossip, anyway," Doug said.

"I know," Mara answered, "But be careful not to go too far the other way and make her out to be a saint either. That wouldn't be fair to Erin."

"I know you're right," Doug agreed. "I wish you could be here to help me."

"I think you'll do fine," Mara said. "My being there would just complicate things. I would love to meet her later, though."

"I'll make sure you do, Doug answered. "The other reason I want to spend a couple of days here, is that I want to make sure that Ellie gets Anna moved in with a friend, that Ben's got the ranch secure—and it looks like he does, and I want to talk more with Ken Tandry about everything that's been happening."

"You have to do whatever you think is best," Mara agreed.

"Then I'll follow up on those things, and call you in two days. You're staying put there for now, right?" he asked Mara

"Yes, for now," she answered. "Joe kind of suggested that it would be a good idea."

"Then that's good enough for me," he replied. "I love you, Mara. Bye."

"I love you, too," she said before hanging up.

CHAPTER THIRTY-TWO

Surprise

WHEN MARA STEPPED INTO THE LOBBY OF THE OLD HOTEL IN CORDOVA, she could barely contain her excitement at seeing Doug standing there.

"But you said you would be in Palmer for two more days," she told him. "I can't believe you're really here!"

"I decided it could wait—all of it," he answered. "Is it too late for you to check out? If it is, we'll just pay up. I got us a room in a boarding house that a friend of mine owns near the harbor."

"Okay, or we could just stay here…" but Mara quickly abandoned her suggestion midsentence, when she looked past Doug and saw Thor standing in the doorway. "Thor's here, too?"

Running to the wolf hybrid that had been Doug's dog since puppyhood, she leaned over as Thor put his paws on her shoulders and licked her face. "It's great to see you, Thor. Come here. Come on. Let me hug you. Come on."

"I can't believe you're here and that you brought Thor with you," Mara continued. "It's like we're almost back to normal again."

"I decided he needed to be with us," Doug said. "It wasn't going to work out with Anna moving down to a friend's house for a while, and with Sarah so close to delivery. Besides, I've been missing my buddy, Thor."

Thor walked over to Doug, moving his body in a slight wiggle and nuzzling his head against the outside of Doug's leg. Mara walked to them, and hugged her husband, prompting Thor to jump up on his hind legs and join in on the group hug.

"This is the best surprise I've had in weeks," Mara said. "I've really missed Thor."

"What about me?" Doug asked, pretending to look hurt.

"I guess I've missed you, too," Mara laughed, throwing her arms around her husband's neck.

It was the first time she had laughed in weeks. For a moment, both of them forgot all about the series of mishaps that had lead to the demise of the *Fire Ring Roamer,* and that now had them in fear for their safety, and possibly even their lives.

"I don't know how you feel about this, Mara, and I know the timing is bad, but…" Doug hesitated, trying to choose his words carefully, "well, I want Thor to be with us and not up with Anna anymore. I mean, for long trips where we're working, maybe she will watch him for us, but we're his pack and he's been with me since he was a pup, and—"

"I want him with us, too, Doug," Mara said. "There's no question about it. I love Thor and I love you. I just can't believe you're both here!"

"Hear that, Thor? You're back home now," she said to their dog.

The hotel desk clerk watched them, suppressing a smile as he tried to find a way to tell them that no dogs were allowed inside. Alaskans were pretty liberal about such rules, but he only worked there and he needed his job. Before the situation could become awkward, Doug went up to him and settled up Mara's bill.

"He's a wolf hybrid, isn't he?" the clerk asked.

"That he is," Doug answered.

Wolf hybrids were fairly common in Alaska and there had been very few documented instances of problems with them. On the contrary, most owners found them to be loyal and affectionate, if not highly intelligent pets. Although Alaska laws were fairly relaxed, Palmer laws were unusually stiff regarding ownership. Doug had obtained the necessary permit and microchip to make Thor legal no matter where he lived in the state, and had also added Mara, Ellie and Anna to the list of Thor's owners.

"He's a beautiful animal," the clerk said as Doug led Thor outside.

"Thanks, man," Doug answered. "They don't come any better than this guy. We'll just wait outside, here, for my wife to get her things."

Mara returned with her bag a few minutes later and the two of them, with Thor trailing behind on a loosely held leash, followed.

The boardinghouse was right on the waterfront and their room was on the bottom floor facing the harbor. Everything about the setting reminded them of their times sleeping on the *Roamer* in Homer harbor, only this time there was no rocking motion to lull them to sleep. After having been apart for the better part of two weeks, though, they really didn't notice. At last they were together, and for these next few days in Cordova, at least, life could be normal again.

CHAPTER THIRTY-THREE

Cordova

ALTHOUGH DOUG HAD BROUGHT HIS TRUCK OVER ON THE FERRY FROM Whittier so that Thor could come along, he and Mara let it sit idle near the boardinghouse. Instead of driving, they walked everywhere around town, usually with Thor ambling along behind them. By all appearances, they were just another couple of fishermen in town for a few days.

Thor was up to his old tricks, too, jumping off the dock into the water every time he saw a fish jump. At least twice Doug found himself explaining the animal's impulsive playfulness to authorities when they handed him warning citations for having his dog unleashed.

"He's usually under real good voice control," Doug insisted to one potbellied official who remained unconvinced.

Finally, Mara found a retractable leash and a combo collar that let Thor feel he was running free while still under Doug's direct control.

"You'll have to keep it together till we leave this town," she told Thor. "Someday we'll find you your own beach to live on, and you can jump in the water all day long if you want to."

"He's gonna hold you to that," Doug told her, after overhearing her words to Thor.

"I hope he does," Mara answered.

When they departed for Haines a few days later, both Doug and Mara vowed to return to Cordova. They agreed, though, that if they ever did find their own beach paradise, it would likely be somewhere with fewer people.

While Mara stayed in their stateroom trying to get over a sinus headache she had developed earlier that day, Doug stayed on the outer deck, watching for the whales he heard had been spotted in the area by a couple of tourists.

Sure enough, about fifteen minutes after moving to the side of the ferry facing the open water, a pod of six orcas began swimming alongside them.

"Those two with the big fins are males, "he told a little girl standing with her mother beside him. When one of the whales snatched a seal off an ice floe, he got a clear look at the gray marking behind the huge dorsal fin and knew they were transient orcas, as opposed to the less aggressive resident orcas that also populated coastal Alaska.

"Seal didn't have a chance," said an old man standing beside Doug.

Doug nodded in agreement before turning to see a short, older Native man, wearing dark glasses and a ball cap standing beside him.

Instinctively he knew.

"You're Joe Michael, aren't you?"

"One and the same," the man answered. "And you're the guy who married the woman who trips on the ferry, aren't you?"

"That I am," Doug answered, remembering how Joe had referred to Mara in that manner in his letter delivered to her in Homer—the one that included the ferry tickets.

"That's Graveyard Island coming up," Joe said.

"I recognize it," Doug answered, moving to the opposite side of the ferry as it came within about 75 feet of the shoreline.

The tide was moving in as the ferry slowed alongside the island. Doug recognized the gravel beach from when he and Mara had attended the memorial for Joe there—this Joe—the one standing right beside him, and who was most definitely not dead.

At least six totem poles of varying heights and ages lined the area between the high tide line and the thick forest of Sitka spruce that covered the small island.

"I see your totem is still standing," he said to Joe.

"It's a fine one, too," Joe said.

"Do the people here—do they know—you know—that you're still alive?" Doug asked him.

"Naw. They think I'm dead," Joe answered. "Every once in a while someone'll be standing on the beach and look at me kinda strange as we pass by. I just go with it. I heard there's a story going around that my spirit appears on the ferry whenever it passes my totem," Joe said. "Part of the legend, you know. Why ruin a good legend by lettin' folks know I'm still around? This way they can remember what they want to about me."

Doug looked at the old man. "But it seemed so real when Mara and I were here for your memorial," he said.

"I know," Joe answered. "I thought so, too."

"You were here?" Doug asked.

"Yeah, I was right over there in the shadows," he answered.

"And no one knew?" Doug asked, amazed at what he was hearing.

"Nope. Not a soul—pardon the pun," Joe chuckled.

"But the aurora, the red dot, the feather…" Doug said, craning his neck to look around an upcoming curve of the island.

"Kinda makes you wonder, doesn't it?" Joe winked.

When Doug turned back around, Joe was gone. On the deck was a small envelope held down with a rock. Doug stooped to pick it up, opened it and read the note inside.

> You got the two tickets
>
> You're both safe with me
>
> Your worry's not over
>
> Trust only the sea.

Doug stood in the thick fog and watched a few passengers depart the ferry in Hoonah. Was that Joe Michael going down the gangway? It looked like it could be the old man, but in the fog he couldn't be sure.

What the…? Was that a red flash coming from Graveyard Island or were his eyes playing tricks on him? There it was again—right near the end of that row of totems—right about where Joe's totem stood—and right about where he remembered both the totem and the red dot painted on the carved feather that ran alongside it.

The ferry had turned away from the dock, obscuring Doug's view of the island. Walking quickly to the rear of the vessel, he strained to see through the fog, but all he could see was darkness and all he could hear was the chug of the motor and the gentle splash the ferry made as it moved through the water. When he finally got a look at Graveyard Island again the fog had lifted and there was no sign of lights flashing from the beach, nor was there any sign of Joe Michael.

CHAPTER THIRTY-FOUR

Strange Story

WHEN MARA WOKE UP FROM HER NAP, THE FERRY HAD JUST PULLED OUT of Hoonah. Doug handed her the note from Joe.

"Where did you get this?" she asked him.

"From Joe Michael," he answered.

Mara stared at him in disbelief. "You met him? He's here?"

"*Was* here is more like it," Doug answered. "I'm pretty sure that he was the passenger I saw getting off the ferry in Hoonah."

Putting his arm around Mara's shoulders, he walked with her around the perimeter of the ferry. Slowly, taking pains not to forget one tiny detail of his encounter with Joe, he told her the story—beginning with how he had been watching the orcas when Joe appeared, and ending with seeing Joe disembark the ferry.

"I swear I saw a faint red light flash in the fog from the direction of the red dot on top of the totem on the beach in Hoonah—the one put up as a memorial after Joe died," Doug said.

Mara slipped her hand into Doug's as they walked around the ferry at least three times before an increase in wind and rougher seas forced them inside to the observation room.

"It's not our imagination that we're in danger, Mara. I just feel it."

"I feel it, too," she answered. "It's just that I've been trying not to think of it, hoping I was wrong and that the feeling would go away."

"It's obvious to me that Joe is here to protect you," Doug continued. "What I can't figure out is why or how."

He leaned back in his chair, propping his heels on the back of the empty chair in front of him, while Mara leaned her head against his shoulder. For a long time, they sat there, rocking with the motion of the ferry.

Finally, Mara said softly, "I don't know how afraid to be."

Doug put his arm around her and pulled her more tightly to him.

"First I lose Brad—but not really," Mara began, "and then…"

Doug tightened his arm around Mara's shoulders as if to shield her from the pain of remembering, while he continued to let her talk. Mara was on a roll as the story of her past spilled out of her for the umpteenth time.

Pausing for a moment in the midst of the recollection she said, "It's ridiculous! No one could make this stuff up!"

"It's pretty bizarre for sure," Doug said, "if I hadn't lived it myself, I would think someone was playing with an overactive imagination. Then, when you factor in the whole situation with Joe, it just makes it all the weirder."

Rehashing all the details of the strange set of circumstances that had ultimately brought them together, they talked about things—things, the same old things, over and over again. Things like the unbelievable relationship that had been uncovered between Sarah, Ellie, Dan, Doug and herself. Things like their own strange meeting on the Alaska Highway, and how they had ended up getting married and finding a happiness that they hoped would finally put their troubles behind them.

Things like the recent revelation that Sassy had a daughter no one knew about, and things like that Ben Donaley was not really the pilot/handyman Ellie thought she had hired, but was really Brad's father—long thought dead—but very much alive and working undercover for the IPA.

"It's enough to make you dizzy," Doug said. "Even I can't keep it all straight."

The sound of the ferry's horn and an announcement that they were approaching Juneau broke their conversation.

Gathering up their belongings, they waited along the outer deck with the other passengers for the ferry to dock. They watched as workers jockeyed the ferry into position along the dock and then threw guide ropes tethered to giant tie-up ropes to the workers below. Once the ferry had been anchored to the dock securely, they waited for foot passengers to disembark, before moving down to the car deck to Doug's truck.

It wasn't clear whether Thor was happier to see them both, or happier to just be getting off the ferry, but once they had driven down the off ramp and out past the ferry terminal, he enjoyed one of the best runs he had had in days—providing Doug and Mara with just the distraction they needed to forget about "things."

CHAPTER THIRTY-FIVE

Juneau

DOUG AND MARA HAD BEEN IN JUNEAU FOR TWO DAYS WHEN DOUG GOT the call on his cell phone from Ben Donaley. Mara listened as Doug did little more than intersperse an occasional "yes", or "uh huh" into the conversation. When he hung up, his brow was furrowed and the lighthearted mood of the past two days was gone.

"Ben says that the IPA has become directly involved in advising both the Coast Guard and the International Maritime Organization about the circumstances involving the sinking of the *Roamer*. He said the good news is that he was able to verify my testimony and file the report I submitted to him while I was back in Palmer."

"And the bad news?" Mara asked, somehow knowing there actually was bad news.

"The bad news is that Ben feels one hundred percent certain that our lives are in danger. Not only our lives," he added, "but the lives of Ellie, Anna, and possibly even Ken and Sarah."

"This is crazy!" Mara exclaimed. "How could he possibly know such a thing?"

"Mara, Ben has been with the IPA for most of his adult life—at least according to what he told me—and we did decide to believe him," he reminded her. "He wants me to fly back to Palmer to convince the others to beef up their security. He can't do it himself because he has to protect his own cover. Ellie already knows that someone has tampered with the *Roamer* and that you and I might be in danger, so it shouldn't be too difficult to convince her. She's already taken steps to protect Anna, and Ken certainly knows something is going on. I just have to make sure they're all safe and all on the same page.

"Ben's flying down to pick me up in the morning. Meanwhile, I'm going to move you to another location under your alias of Jane Brown. I'm also going to leave my truck here for you and Thor to use."

"But, Doug—"

"Mara. This really is no surprise, is it?" Doug said. "I know we suspected this, now we know it to be true. According to Ben, no one suspects you are traveling either alone or with a dog, so it should be easy to maintain your cover."

Mara walked away from Doug so he couldn't see the mixture of anger and tears on her face.

"There's no other way, Mara."

"I believe you," she answered softly. "Why wouldn't I believe you? You're my husband and you've been through all of this with me. But," she said, brushing back the tears from her eyes, "you're about the only person I do believe anymore."

Could she really mean those words? Sarah had been her best friend since high school and Ken had been the lead investigator in both Dan's and Brad's murders. It went without saying that Mara adored Ellie and her daughter, Anna.

"Mara, you know you don't mean that," Doug said. "Your friends mean everything to you—and what about old Joe? Hasn't he protected you beyond anything you ever believed was possible?"

"That's another thing," she said, whirling to face Doug. "Who is Joe Michael and why is he always trying to save *me*? Don't you think there's something weird about that? I mean, why me of all people on this earth—a perfect stranger to him when he first handed me the feather—way back before this whole mess began."

Who wouldn't wonder about that? Certainly Doug had asked himself that very question.

"I have often wondered about that myself, Mara," he said after a while. "I really don't know what to say except that I believe Joe is that special person that all of us find in life if we're lucky. Don't get me wrong. I'm not claiming to really understand what is going on with Joe Michael or why he chose you to protect. All I know is that Joe has laid down his life for you and that he was right each time he warned you. Don't doubt him, Mara. His presence is a gift you've been given. Treasure it."

"My heart says you're right, Doug," she answered. "but my mind—it's just all so confusing and so—so hard, so unreal—but, yet, it *is* real."

"We have to keep the faith, Mara," Doug said. "And, one more thing."

Mara glared at him. The frustration inside had risen to the boiling point after they had re-hashed all that had happened. How many "one more things" could she absorb right now? With all the patience she could summon, she listened.

"Ben is bringing Karen Steele with him tomorrow when he picks me up. He wants her to spend a couple of days with you getting to know you and working on a plan to keep you safe."

"Okay," Mara answered.

"I think you can trust her."

"Okay," she answered again.

For the rest of the day they looked for a more secluded location on the outer edge of town—one that had enough activity around to keep her from being too isolated. When they found it, they moved Mara's things there. Afterwards, they went to dinner at a small little bistro down by the docks before turning in early. Who knew how long before they would have a chance to really be together like this again? Morning, as was always the case when she was with Doug, would come all too soon.

CHAPTER THIRTY-SIX

Don't Call Me Beth

From the air, Ben Donaley could see Doug and Mara waiting in Doug's truck next to the private airstrip that he had directed them to. It was early in the morning and a cold fog hugged the ground as if protecting the earth from the intense light of the bright morning sun. It looked like the morning would be clear and warm, just right for a safe landing and take-off, although he was quick to note the thin wisps of clouds slinking midway across the mountains that told of a coming storm.

"Looks like we'll need to leave within the hour to beat the weather, Beth," Ben said to Karen Steele.

"Daddy—Ben—we talked about this. You have to always call me Karen or Miss Steele, lest you slip up and reveal my real identity—and I have to do the same in return and only call you Ben. If they knew you were really Benton Edwards, no telling the amount of danger it would put us all in," Beth Edwards told her father.

"I know, cupcake," Ben told his daughter, unable to resist using the pet name he had used for her as a child.

Karen Steele straightened her skirt and adjusted her bag on her lap, preparing for landing. She purposely turned away from her father and stared out the passenger window in an attempt to regain her demeanor as a top agent of the IPA.

Ben Donaley landed the red and white Cessna with a minimum of bumps, and slowly brought it around to face Doug's truck.

"You take care of Mara, Thor," Doug said, scratching Thor's ears before opening his door and stepping out of his truck. As he walked around to open Mara's door, he called over to Ben. "Morning, Donaley. Couldn't ask for better visibility if you custom-ordered it, could ya?"

"Sure couldn't," Ben responded before turning slightly toward Karen.

"Doug and Mara Williams, you remember IPA agent Karen Steele don't you?"

"Yes I do," Doug answered, extending his hand.

"Nice to see you again," Doug told her. "I trust that my wife will be in good hands—safe hands—under your watch?"

"As safe as two women alone in Juneau can be," Karen Steele smiled wryly. "Please don't worry, Mr. Williams, keeping Mara safe is my top priority right now, rest assured."

Mara smiled slightly. "All three of you talk about me as if I'm not here. I don't know how I've managed to get this far in life without each of you showing me the way."

"Mara, honey..." Doug said, putting his arm around her.

"Seriously, Doug. Isn't it bad enough that all of this is going on without everyone treating me like I'm some kind of delicate, slow-witted waif?"

Ben Donaley busied himself with the plane as Doug shifted uncomfortably and Karen Steele rifled though her bag.

"I'm sure Mrs. Williams and I will be fine, Doug," Karen Steele said. "It will more than likely be me that needs her help since I've never been to Juneau before."

At that moment, Thor took off running after a couple of ducks that had just lifted off from a nearby pond, causing Doug to have to make a short sprint to retrieve him when Thor would not heed the call to return.

"Come here, Thor," Mara said, taking Thor from Doug by the collar and snapping on his leash.

"He always gets disruptive when he knows we're busy," she told Karen Steele.

Turning to her husband, Mara said, "I'm sorry I snapped at you, Doug. It's just that this is all getting to me, too."

"We'll leave you two to say your goodbyes," Ben Donaley said, taking Karen by the arm and leading her to the other side of the plane.

"I want you to try to keep your wits about you, Mara," Doug told his wife. "From here on out, I've got a feeling that things are going to get pretty dicey, and this is no time for you to lose your focus. I'll call you on our secure line the minute we get into Palmer—just to let you know I'm safe. From then on, I'll be calling less often so as to lessen any chance that anyone will overhear me talking to you."

"Okay," Mara answered.

"I want you to keep Thor with you at all times—in the truck, in your room, wherever you are, do you hear me? Wherever you go, Thor goes, okay?"

"Okay," she answered, beginning to lose the fight that had threatened to rise within her at being cast in a dependent position again.

Ben had already started up the plane, leaving Doug and Mara time to do little more than kiss and hug quickly before Doug climbed into the plane for takeoff. Minutes later, Mara and Karen Steele were both waving to the departing plane before, soon, it was almost out of sight.

"How about a cup of coffee?" Karen Steele asked.

"Yeah. Sure. Okay," Mara answered.

With Thor in the truck between them, Mara drove the two of them to one of the local hangouts where they could have an espresso and talk—if that's what her babysitter wanted to do, that was.

CHAPTER THIRTY-SEVEN

Gunfire

THE WINDOW SHATTERED ONLY A FEW FEET FROM WHERE KAREN STEELE and Mara sat in the small espresso shop near the Juneau harbor, but luckily the bullet lodged in the wood frame around the entry to the women's restroom at the back of the store.

While the clerk called 911, customers scrambled to leave the building as another shot rang out, this time sending a bullet through the plastic cone atop one of the commercial coffee grinders used in the shop.

While coffee beans spilled out like the soft hiss of a tiny avalanche, Karen grabbed Mara's arm and pulled her toward the rear exit located down a narrow hallway that also led to the restrooms. Somehow, Thor had broken his leash, because he was right behind Mara with the torn leash dangling behind him.

"I'm not sure if it's me or you they're after," Karen spat out, "but I'm pretty sure it's one of us."

The sound of more bullets ricocheting through the small shop pinged in the background as Karen and Mara, followed by Thor, ran through a marshy area behind the buildings. Karen pulled a .38 revolver out of her pocket and passed it to Mara. "Keep this in your pocket. Just cock it, point it and squeeze the trigger—but only if there's no other choice. And keep your wits about you, Mara. Things could start getting weird."

Karen Steele fingered the 9mm she carried in her other pocket and led Mara toward the marsh.

"Keep an eye out for black bears and wolves, but I'm more worried about people than wild animals," she said.

"Thor, run ahead and watch for bears," Mara told the dog, unhooking what remained of his leash from his collar before sending him on.

They hadn't heard any more shots for several minutes. Away from the tourist area as they now were, the quiet gave them time to calm their nerves.

Mara had to pee. Bottom line. There was no sense trying to pretend otherwise and she said so in as many words to Karen Steele.

"It's the adrenaline," Karen said simply. "I'll wait near that convenience store ahead. There'll be a restroom in there."

The sound of sirens responding to the gunshots permeated the air, and Karen Steele knew that she and Mara were on their own for now. Leaning against the back wall of the convenience store, she closed her eyes for a few seconds to collect her thoughts. Seeing the women stop, Thor doubled back and waited at the door he had seen Mara go into.

"Sure as I'm standin' here, if it ain't you again, Jane," a woman's voice said from the stall next to Mara's.

Mara recognized the voice of the woman who had befriended her in Kodiak. She flushed the toilet and stepped out of the stall before speaking, though—just in case. Sal Kindle stepped out of her stall next, and stood next to Mara at the sink.

"Sal?" Mara said answering her own question as she spoke. "This is really weird. What in the world are you doing in Juneau?"

"Flew in last night," Sal answered. "I'm meetin' up with my old man over in Hoonah tonight. I told you about him."

"What you didn't tell me was that it was Joe Michael," Mara answered.

"So you figured it out, did ya?" Sal answered.

"Joe told me," Mara replied.

"Just like a man to spit everything out like that," Sal said. "But, such is the way of love, Jane. You would know that as much as anyone."

"Look, Sal, I'm in some kind of trouble and I'm not sure how or why. A friend and I—at least I think she's a friend—are running from someone who just tried to kill us."

"I heard the sirens," Sal said, nodding.

"I'd like to chat, but I gotta go," Mara said.

"Before you do," Sal said, putting one hand on Mara's elbow to hold her back, "I want you ta listen up."

Reaching into her pocket, Sal pulled out a single key that was attached to an old shower ring. "This is the key to my trailer house just outside of town, here, okay? I want ya to go there. No one's gonna ask any questions and if they do, tell 'em yer house-sittin' for me. Same story, yer my cousin Jane from Peoria. I'll be back in town in a coupla days."

"But, what about…what if…" Mara stuttered.

"Feel free to take yer friend out there with ya, Jane. If you say she's okay, then I say she's okay, and she looks okay to me—though she seems to be a bit of a tight…well, ya know what I mean.

"And it goes without sayin' that yer wolf-dog don't need no invitation. If yer loved by a wolf-dog like it seems you are, then he's more deservin' to stay inside than a good percentage of people I met in my life."

Before Mara could say anymore, Sal opened the door and disappeared.

CHAPTER THIRTY-EIGHT

Beth Revealed

MARA AND THOR WERE A GOOD MILE OUT OF TOWN BEFORE KAREN STEELE caught up with them.

"What do you think you're doing, Mara?" Karen said in a voice that was surprisingly even.

Thor leaned up against Mara's leg and laid his ears back as Karen spoke.

"I've got some place to be," Mara answered, reaching into her jacket pocket with one hand and holding onto Thor's collar with the other.

"I wouldn't make any sudden moves with that gun if I were you," Agent Steele said, placing her hand on Mara's right arm to keep her from pulling anything out of her pocket.

Thor let out a rumbling growl, which prompted Karen Steele to let go of Mara's arm.

Mara fingered the gun she had stuffed in her pocket as she pulled away. "I'm just trying to give you your gun back. I don't want it. I don't want you here. I can take care of myself."

"Look, Mara, don't do this," Karen said.

"Don't do what?" Mara answered.

"Stop it, Mara!" Karen said, her voice taking on a sharper tone. "Stop it. This is no time to mess around. You're in danger. We're both in danger. Stop acting like a fool."

"No one was shooting at me before you showed up. Why should I get all hung up in some drama you and the IPA have going on?" Mara sniped, pulling back on Thor's collar to keep him from moving toward Karen Steele.

"Don' be stupid, Mara. This isn't a game. Whoever it was, was shooting at both of us," Karen said.

"So you say," Mara shot back.

"Look, Mara," Karen said, choosing her words carefully. "I can't blame you for feeling the way you do. If I were in your shoes, I would probably feel the same way."

"You don't know me from Adam," Mara said. "And you don't know what I think. All you know is that you got stuck babysitting me and I don't need or want a babysitter. I've been doing fine so far without you."

Karen Steele was beginning to lose patience.

"Give me the gun, Mara."

Mara handed her the .38, which Karen stuffed into her own pocket before walking ahead of Mara away from town.

"Suit yourself, Mrs. Williams," she said. "If you don't want the protection of the IPA, then go on back into town and take your chances that no one was shooting at you."

Karen Steele continued walking away.

"My guess, though, is that most of the attitude you're directing at me is a result of your own realization that everything I told you is true. You're in danger, your husband's in danger, and your friends are in danger—and you know it."

Mara took her cell phone out of her other pocket and began to dial Doug's number.

"I wouldn't do that if I were you," Karen Steele looked back and told her. "Not unless you want to call attention to your whereabouts."

Mara stopped dialing and put the phone back in her pocket. She knew the IPA agent was right. Both Ben Donaley and Doug had warned her about using the cell phone. As much as she didn't like it, she had no choice but to follow Karen Steele out of town.

"I'm gonna have to figure out a place for us to stay," Agent Steele told her.

"I've got a safe place for us to stay," Mara said. "It's a trailer house that's about another mile down this road if I got the directions right."

Mara released her grasp on Thor's collar and let Thor run off ahead, watching as the dog occasionally circled back as if to keep a close watch on her. She reached for the torn scrap of paper that Sal had handed to her in the bathroom at the convenience store. If they were on the right track, that would be Sal's white trailer with the light green shutters and door right down the road and to the left.

"Well, isn't that interesting," Karen Steele replied when Mara showed her the map.

"Look," Mara said, tiring of the hostile exchange of words, "if we're stuck together like glue, then I might as well try to get along with you, after all, you did offer me some support when my first husband was killed and you claim you were looking out for me way back when. I guess for that, I owe you—and I guess for that, I'm gonna have to believe you really are here for my own good."

Karen Steele slowed her pace and waited for Mara to catch up.

"I met someone in the restroom—someone who has helped me before," Mara said, going on to explain the story of how Sal Kindle had befriended her in Kodiak, but leaving out the part about Joe Michael and the feather. That story, she was certain, a hardened agent like Karen Steele would never understand.

"Okay. She sounds okay," Karen replied. "There's a lot of those types here in Alaska—strangers who'll see a person in need and give 'em a hand. She sounds like one of those."

"Sal's okay," Mara assured her, going on to explain how Sal had intervened with the hotel owner. "Sal gave me these directions. This is her trailer house. She keeps it for when she's in Juneau."

Holding up the scrap of paper that Sal had given her in the restroom, Mara looked at the crudely drawn directions again.

"If I'm reading this right, then that's Sal's trailer up beyond and to the left."

Karen Steele let Mara take the lead as they walked the quarter of a mile or so on the dirt road that led to the trailer. Why was she even here? Why hadn't she just put in for her leave instead of accepting this assignment? She could be relaxing right now—picking out cakes and flowers and dresses, instead of traipsing around Alaska one step ahead of a pack of thugs and lowlifes, protecting people who didn't even know what kind of danger they were in, much less appreciating that she was keeping them out of harm's way.

How weird life was. Vint Mariah had been her brother's best friend and, for a while, his partner in the IPA. If someone hadn't taken his life, Brad would surely have been the best man at their upcoming wedding, and this ornery woman she was protecting would more than likely have been in the wedding party. For that reason only, she would persevere—for Brad—because this was the woman he had loved more than she ever knew.

"My brother would have been proud of you," she blurted out.

"What did you say?" Mara said.

"My brother," Karen said. "Your husband, Brad."

Mara dropped the keys she had been preparing to use to unlock the door to Sal's trailer.

"That's right," Karen told her. "My name is Beth Edwards and Ben Donaley is my father."

"Here, Thor," Mara called to her dog as she picked up the keys and let them all inside.

CHAPTER THIRTY-NINE

Momentary Affection

"I'VE GOT DOUG ON THE PHONE," KAREN STEELE SAID TO MARA LATER that evening after the two sisters-in-law had had a chance to absorb the impact of the news that Karen Steele was really Brad's sister, Beth Edwards.

Mara took the phone into a back room to talk and quickly learned that on the flight back to Palmer, Ben Donaley had already told Doug the story about who Karen Steele really was.

Doug had been gone for less than a day and already so much had changed.

"It's like a nightmare that won't end," she told him, recounting the shooting that had sent her and Karen Steele fleeing from the coffee shop, along with the surprise encounter with Sal.

"Yes, Thor's fine. Somehow he broke his leash from where I had him tied up outside the coffee shop and he came running right to me. I know he was supposed to be with me, but they wouldn't let him inside so I tied him where I could see him. He's right here beside me. I know he hates gunshots since he got shot. He's fine—really. No, I won't make that mistake again."

"Thank God you have a safe place to stay," Doug told her, trying not to let his voice reveal the intense worry he felt for her safety. "Don't worry about the room I rented for you. I'll settle up the bill with them. It's good that you had your backpack and all your things with you. Put the phone up to Thor's ear so I can talk to him, okay?"

Mara held the phone to Thor's ear, watching him perk up his ears and then lick the phone, before she took it back to talk with Doug herself.

"He said he feels better hearing your voice," Mara said.

Reaching down, she stroked Thor's head as she continued to talk with her husband.

"You know, in a way," Mara said, "Some things are now starting to make sense—sort of like the pieces of a puzzle coming together."

Doug had to agree at least, in part. There were still too many unknowns, though. Like who had sabotaged his boat—and why? And what was Sassy's daughter doing in Palmer when a few months ago no one even knew she existed? And who had killed Sassy? Why had Joe Michael faked his own death, and who was this woman named Sal Kindle that kept popping up to help Mara? Until these questions were answered, he couldn't trust that anything was real right now. This life of living on the run had gotten old about two days after it began.

"All I know is that Ben Donaley seems like a straight-up man," He told Mara, "and I think his story about being Brad's father, as bizarre as it sounds, makes sense. I like the man."

Doug hesitated a bit before continuing, "I want to trust him, Mara. I do trust him, but I belong with you. I need to find a way to convince Ben that we won't be in any more danger together than we are apart."

"Yes," I agree he's telling the truth," Mara said. "I can even see a little of Brad in his face, and Karen—I mean Beth—seems genuine, too."

Mara went on to explain how she and Beth had spent the last two hours talking—mostly about Brad and their childhood.

"There's a picture of them together—they were about nine and ten then," she said. "Brad had the same picture of the two of them in his wallet. Beth had one for each year after that until Brad left for college when he was eighteen. Looking at those pictures, there is no mistaking that she is the same person."

A sudden cloudburst broke up the signal causing them to have to hurriedly say goodbye, but not before Mara told her husband that as much as she trusted both Ben and his daughter, Beth, she would feel safe only when she was with him again.

"I'll take good care of Thor and he'll take good care of me. I love you. Bye," she said.

By the time Mara had returned to the living room, golf-ball-sized hail was hammering the metal roof of the trailer. Pulling the curtain back, she watched the raining ice balls pile up on the small patch of grass that passed for a lawn outside the front entry.

"It's lucky you found this place for us," Beth said. "I wouldn't want to be trying to hunker down somewhere outside in this mess."

Earlier, after revealing who she really was, Beth had told Mara she had been planning on taking a leave from the IPA to plan her own wedding. The situation with Sassy's murder had changed all that—at least for now.

"Let's talk about something happy. Tell me about your wedding plans," Mara said to her.

Beth did just that. She told Mara about Vint, and how he and Brad had been best friends in IPA training camp, and ever since. At one point, she pulled Vint's picture out of her purse and showed it to her sister-in-law. Mara was happy she didn't recognize him. At least there would be no new surprises here.

"He's very cute," she told Beth, amused to see the tough IPA agent blush.

"I probably shouldn't even be showing this to you, Mara," Beth said. "Don't tell Ben or he'll have a fit."

Mara was unaccustomed to seeing the woman she knew as an IPA agent behaving this normally. She stroked Thor's head gently as she and Beth talked.

"I promise you that I won't do anything to reveal that I have ever laid eyes on this man before," she told Beth, laughing.

Taking on a more serious tone, she said, "Believe me, I know what it's like to want to protect the man you love, and how the longing to be together leaves you feeling so vulnerable and alone."

"I've told you more than I should have," Beth said, also taking on a more serious tone.

"From now on, you're going to need to refer to me only as Karen or Miss Steele. If I'm to work effectively to protect you, then you cannot ever let your guard down, even when you think it's safe. I'm depending on you to help protect my identity, Mara. At this point, outside of Doug, Ben, and your friends Ellie and Sarah and their families, there's no one—and I mean no one, that we can trust."

"I understand," Mara said. "I won't let you down."

"Thank you, "agent Steele replied, taking on her former demeanor, and leaving Mara to wonder if the last two days had even really happened.

Revealing one last glimpse of who she really was, Karen Steele added gently, "We'll do all we can to get you and Doug together again. Lucky you have Thor, here, too."

CHAPTER FORTY

Haines

WHEN MARA DROVE DOUG'S TRUCK UP THE RAMP ONTO THE *MALASP-na*, memories of her move to Alaska a little over one year ago came flooding back. Then, she had been a widow who had finally come to terms with the death of the only man she had ever loved. Now, she was married to someone even more wonderful than the man she had lost, and was embroiled in a mystery decidedly more bizarre than the one that had brought them together.

As the ferry workers tied her truck securely to the safety loops that rose from the cement floor of the car deck of the ferry, she leaned over and hugged Thor before making sure that the bowl of water she had left for him on the floor had not tipped over.

"I know you'd rather stretch out in the truck bed," she told him, "but we all know what an escape artist you are, and no telling what you might take off after if you get a mind to."

Thor laid his head on Mara's arm and looked at her with the most pitiful look his dog eyes could express.

"You forgot how cold and damp it is down here," Mara told him, backing slowly out of the truck. "You just toughen up and I'll see you on the next car deck call."

Mara closed the door and walked away without looking back. She had to. There was no other way she could stand to leave Thor behind like this. Besides, she doubted there would even be a car deck call on this short trip from Juneau to Haines.

When she stepped through the door to the stairwell, she forced herself to think of her trip plan, her next meal, anything but the sad look on Thor's face. Once up on the main deck, she walked slowly around and watched as the *Malaspina* pulled away from the ferry terminal in Juneau.

On the docks below, she could see Karen Steele, dressed in the navy blue pencil skirt and white blouse uniform of the IPA, talking intently with a man dressed in navy pants and a white shirt. She watched them part ways, as he walked toward town with a navy blue jacket slung over one arm, and carrying a black briefcase. About a block farther down, he got into a black SUV and drove off.

In the other direction, she saw Karen Steele duck into the same convenience store where they had come under fire. A few minutes later, she emerged, wearing jeans, knee-high rubber boots, and a tattered sweater, making her blend perfectly with the local population. Somewhere in the tote bag that likely held the professional clothes she had just shed, Karen Steele carried Mara's note for Sal Kindle thanking her for the safe refuge of the past few days.

Dear Sal,

> How do you thank someone who appears as though a guardian angel sent from heaven, and who is there to shield you from unsuspected harm not just once, but twice? Please accept my heartfelt gratitude for your friendship.

Jane

Once they were tied up in Haines two and a half hours later, Mara went down to the car deck, where she was surprised to find Joe Michael just getting out of her truck.

"How in the world did you get in my truck—let alone not get caught by the ferry workers? And what is going on? Thor, are you okay?" she said looking past Joe to check on her dog.

"No biggie," Joe answered. "I was just walking by and Thor said he wanted out, so I took him for a walk."

"But how did you get in? The truck was locked. How come the engine is running? You don't have a key—" Mara spat out in astonishment.

"Don't freak out," Joe said in his quiet monotone, while Thor just looked at her as if there was no reason for all the panic.

"But—" Mara began.

"Look, like I said, it's no biggie."

"But, how?" Mara said.

"Learned it in Nam," Joe answered, as much to silence her as to inform. "I was just bringing you back Sal's thanks for the thank-you note. Now I gotta go. See ya."

Mara reached down and picked up the note Joe had left on the seat of her truck. Unfolding the small sheet of notepaper, she read:

> Don't let my man scare ya, Jane. By now you gotta know he's the best. Safe trip. *Sal*

Minutes later, Mara and Thor were driving down the off ramp into Haines—only, unlike the last time she was here, this time it was spring. Also, unlike the last time, this time she would drive the nearly 500 miles straight to Tok—anything to avoid staying at either Destruction Bay or the Beaver Creek Lodge again.

142

CHAPTER FORTY-ONE

Carlos Returns

DOUG WILLIAMS TENSED AS HE FELT THE COLD METAL PRESS AGAINST THE back of his neck.

"First you sleep with the mother and then the daughter?" A man speaking with a Spanish accent hissed.

When Doug flinched, the man holding the gun to his neck grabbed him by his right arm and twisted it behind his back.

"You sorry—" Doug winced.

"Don't try anything stupid, man. Your life means nothing to me now and it will mean even less when I can be sure you don't know the location of the money."

"I don't know anything about any money," Doug growled, "and I'm not sleeping—"

"Shut up!" the man snapped, twisting Doug's arm more tightly against his back. "A.C. warned me about you and how you always like to play dumb about everything. I oughta just off you now and get it over with, but first—"

"Put the gun down, Carlos," Erin De la Corte yelled from the dining room window of the house she had inherited from Sassy.

Held tightly to her shoulder was her mother's shotgun, aimed squarely at the man who had formerly been her live-in lover.

"You should've never left me, Erin, baby," Carlos said, lowering the gun from Doug's neck but still maintaining his grip on his arm.

"And you should have told me you were married, Carlos," Erin said.

"Ah, Erin. Imelda told me the two of you had met. Shame on her for spilling the beans. She knows better," he answered in a singsong voice that made Erin cringe.

"Imelda only told me the truth, Carlos, and exposed your lies," Erin continued.

"She has learned not to do such a thing again," Carlos sneered.

Carlos' sinister tone sent chills through Erin, prompting her to tighten her grip on the shotgun.

"Imelda was right about you, Carlos. You are a pig," Erin defied him, overcoming the trembling she felt inside to keep the shotgun pointed at him. "Let my friend go. He knows nothing of any of this."

Carlos shoved Doug to the ground and whirled around, pointing his pistol squarely at Erin.

"Erin! Duck!" Ethan Shepherd yelled from inside the house, pushing Erin away from the window.

Reflexively, Erin did just that, screaming before fainting, as Ethan's bloody form fell in slow motion in front of her.

By the time she came to, someone had moved her to the sofa. In front of her, near the window, lay a sheet-covered human form. Two uniformed police officers were in the process of directing the coroner to the body.

"Ethan?" she whispered in a voice that verged on hysteria.

"Ethan saved you from Carlos' bullet," Doug told her.

Erin began trembling and Doug put his arms around her as she began to sob. He was more than shaken himself. Why was it so hard to stop his own trembling? Why couldn't Mara be here with him? If it weren't so unsafe, she would be. He fought back the anger that had so easily surfaced lately. Why was there always somebody who needed comforting? Was there no end to the constant, unrelenting heartbreak?

"We've contacted Don Shepherd about his son," one of the officers told them. "He's making arrangements to have the body shipped back to California."

"Some…some…one…someone…" Erin was wracked with sobs, unable to finish her sentence.

Doug stood up, his face perfectly concealing the turmoil playing out inside his head. An officer told him that the gunman had escaped and asked if he knew anything about who he was? Could he provide a description of the perpetrator?

"His name is Carlos. That's what Erin—Miss De la Corte—called him. Carlos," Doug told them, proceeding to describe the clothes Carlos was wearing and his impression of his height, weight, and hair color, "and he was clean-shaven."

"I know this for sure because I noticed a large scar on his chin—and he wore a ruby ring on the little finger of his right hand—you know, a pinkie ring."

"We're going to need to talk to her as soon as she is able," one of the officers said as he looked in Erin's direction.

"I don't think…" Doug tried to tell them. "Well, I don't think anyone else lives here but the two of them—you know, Erin and Ethan—I mean, except for Stan, the caretaker, but he lives in the barn."

"She's gonna need someone to watch her," on officer said, glancing in Erin's direction.

"I'll stay for now," Doug answered. "Until we can figure something out."

Doug listened while the officer told him they had put out an all-points bulletin alerting Alaskan and Canadian police that a man going by the name of Carlos had held one person hostage and murdered another, before escaping on foot sometime around two that afternoon.

"We'll get him," they assured Doug. "No doubt about that."

Before Doug could comment, an Officer Denton spoke up, "The man is obviously armed and dangerous. No telling what he's capable of after this."

Erin raised herself from the sofa and walked slowly to where the men were standing. Through the tears that were still streaming down her face, she finished what she had been trying to say earlier, "Someone needs to get ahold of Michael."

"What is his relationship to the deceased?" Officer Denton asked her.

"Stop calling him 'the deceased'" Erin snapped. "His name is Ethan and he's a person!"

"I'm sorry, ma'am. Just trying to do my job," Officer Denton said.

"Michael Opelson is Ethan's life-partner," Erin told him. "And Michael's father is Garner Opelson, candidate for governor of California."

"And one more thing, officer," Erin said, "You should know before talking to them that neither Ethan's nor Michael's family know about their relationship. Ethan wanted it that way. He didn't think they would understand if they knew. He and Michael were very private people."

After providing the officers with Michael's contact information, she said, "Please, could you let me be the one to tell Michael? And could someone call my parents?"

CHAPTER FORTY-TWO

Palmer Police... Again

THE NEXT MORNING, ERIN AND DOUG SAT BEFORE SERGEANT JAMES AT the Palmer Police Department while Erin explained her relationship with the man who had murdered Ethan Shepherd.

Referring to Ken Tandry, Sergeant James began, "Ken assures me that your word is above reproach, Mr. Williams. It's important for you to understand that you are being questioned as a witness to a murder and are not under suspicion yourself."

"Thank you," Doug answered, grateful for the reassurance.

"I know Ken needed to be home right now with the baby due any day now," Doug said, "and I appreciate that he put a competent man such as yourself on this case. Whatever I can do to help you catch this guy, Carlos—I'll do it. It makes you wonder if the series of suspicious things going on around those of us who knew Sassy and A.C. is somehow connected."

Watching Sergeant James type his information into a computer, Doug added, "Never in my wildest dreams did I think that I would be caught up in this mess of violence that seems to have become my life for the past year or two."

Sergeant James continued to type. Doug leaned back in his chair, while Erin fidgeted with something in her purse, eventually locating a tube of lipgloss that she absently applied to her lips.

Sergeant James typed for several more minutes before turning to face Erin.

"On the other hand, you, Miss De la Corte, are wanted in both Mexico and California for unpaid traffic violations amounting to some two thousand dollars. And..." he paused for emphasis, "and apparently you were stopped on the Palmer Wasilla Highway last week for both speeding and illegal passing."

"I can explain the incident in Palmer," Erin said, standing up. "I was on my way to the hospital because I was having an allergic reaction to some shellfish I had just eaten for lunch. I believe the officer told me he was going to put that in the report."

"Yes, he did make a statement to that effect," Sergeant James said. "I assume you will be able to provide us with your emergency room records for additional confirmation, then?"

"Yes, of course," Erin replied. "And those other tickets—Carlos told me he took care of them."

Erin began crying, grabbing onto Doug's arms and looking at him with a look of pleading distress. "I believed him. Carlos lied to me and now he murdered Ethan. I can't believe this is happening!"

"I believe the Carlos that you are referring to is Carlos Luis Antoya. Is that correct, Miss De la Corte?" Ben Donaley said from the doorway.

"I'll take over now," he said to Sergeant James, flashing his IPA badge as he spoke. "Carlos Antoya is wanted as the henchman of an international drug-smuggling operation between Mexico, Canada and the United States. We have reason to believe that he has recently crossed paths with the leaders of the South American cartel, and that Mr. Williams and Miss De la Corte are being targeted by both factions through their link to Amanda 'Sassy' Carlson and her deceased brother A.C."

Neither Doug nor Erin said anything, each unsure as to how they figured in to such an elaborate connection.

Erin was the first to speak. "I'm going to need to talk to my lawyer."

"As well you should, Miss De la Corte," Ben Donaley said. "And you should probably consider getting one yourself, Doug, because this case promises to be so big that I cannot guarantee your complete protection from all that the investigation is going to uncover."

Doug bristled and shot a puzzled look Ben Donaley's way.

"I'm not saying you're being accused or are going to be accused of anything, Doug," Ben continued. "I'm just saying that this is big and I want—on the most personal level—for your rights to be fully protected."

Taking Doug aside as Sergeant James talked briefly with Erin, Ben Donaley said, "And Mara should get someone, too. I'll make sure that Karen Steele follows up with her, although the last I heard, Mara was on her way up the Alcan, heading for Palmer."

"If you just sign this report, I'll release it to Mr. Donaley and the IPA now," Sergeant James told Doug, not giving him a chance to react to the news about Mara.

Doug signed as instructed and handed the report back to Sergeant James before walking out the door behind Ben Donaley.

"I guess I'll be seeing more of you," he told Erin De la Corte as he walked past her. "I'm just not sure—aside from the obvious crime spree—why that scares me."

CHAPTER FORTY-THREE

Ben and Doug

DOUG WALKED OUT OF THE POLICE STATION WITH BEN DONALEY. IN THE BACK-ground, he could hear Sergeant James reading Erin De la Corte her rights.

"It seems like Erin got a raw deal from Carlos," Doug said.

"Don't be too worried about her arrest," Donaley answered. "First off, she'll be safer in jail until Carlos Antoya gets brought in, and second off, her parents are on their way here from Santa Barbara with her lawyer to straighten this all out. I believe that once she pays off the fines, the charges will be dropped—especially in exchange for any information she has about Carlos Antoya."

"It's good that someone will be here to look out for her. She seems pretty vulnerable right now," Doug said.

"You're pretty vulnerable yourself right now," Ben said. "You need to watch your back."

"I'll be fine," Doug replied.

"Don't get cocky, Doug," Ben answered. "All the tampering incidents with your seiner, Mara and Karen Steele getting shot at, the fire at Erin's Palmer ranch—it's all starting to look connected. Then there's the report about Erin's father getting beaten up in his own stable in Santa Barbara—Carlos actually claimed responsibility for that one—all of it is starting to point to some connection involving both Carlos and the Mexican cartel, and maybe even the Brazilian cartel."

Doug listened as Ben continued, "I cannot impress on you strongly enough, just how dangerous and ruthless Carlos Antoya and others connected with him are. If our intelligence proves accurate, things will be coming to a head very soon."

"But how could I possibly be involved?" he asked. "Or Mara?"

"We have reason to believe," Ben Donaley replied, "that A.C. was working both the Mexican and South American drug cartels, and that neither cartel was aware of his involvement with the other until just before his death."

"Next you're going to tell me that this somehow ties into my brother Dan's death." Doug said.

"I think it does. Just the fact that Steve Bitten moved to Oregon made A.C. suspicious. He either suspected that Dan was serving as a liaison between Steve and the cartels as his Alaska connection, or that Steve was splitting his take with Dan to somehow benefit the business—forgive his own debt, maybe.

"My son died by A.C.'s hand working undercover as your brother's business partner Steve Bitten. Not only was Brad one of our best agents, but as you already know, he was my son. He was also Mara's loving husband until he disappeared to protect her.

"A.C.'s own demise at the hand of his sister, Sassy, ultimately sealed her fate, too, if as we suspect, the cartels believe she killed her own brother to get his money."

"But Sassy loved A.C.," Doug said. "She would never kill him for his money. No one who knows her would ever believe that."

"We think the Mexican cartel, on learning of A.C.'s death, came looking for a large payoff that was due them from him, and that they suspected that Sassy knew where the money was hidden. Apparently they were unable to find what they wanted, either because she couldn't or wouldn't tell them. That would explain Sassy's murder."

"But how does that involve Erin?" Doug asked. "Or me? Or Mara?"

"It's pure coincidence that Sassy's illegitimate daughter was the one woman of all the mistresses tied to Carlos Antoya that he could not let go. It's even stranger that Carlos happened to be the person in the huge Mexican cartel designated to find A.C.'s hidden money. We believe that Carlos and his men found Sassy while Carlos was looking for Erin and that the fact that Erin was Sassy's daughter came as quite a surprise to him, even causing him to believe that Erin had betrayed him not only in love, but by hiding money he felt was his," Ben Donaley explained.

"But Erin—did she even know?" Doug asked.

"From what we've been able to ascertain, she didn't have a clue," Donaley said. "Not about A.C., not about Carlos, not about any of it. She was in Palmer only to settle her mother's estate."

"If I hadn't lived this, I would never believe it," Doug said. "Even now it's almost impossible to understand. How does the South American cartel figure in?"

"We're not sure how they figure in this time," Ben said as he paced back and forth a few times and wiped his forehead with a kerchief before continuing. "We know they figured in Dan's murder, but we're not sure whether or not they figure in Sassy's murder, especially since A.C. is no longer in the picture.

"Look, Doug, I'm only telling you all this because I trust you implicitly. I've watched the way you look after Mara and have seen how much you love her. Now that my own son can't take care of her anymore, I can only thank God you were sent to be her husband."

Doug saw a rare glimpse of emotion flash across Ben Donaley's face and knew the man was sincere. Thankfully, Ben Donaley couldn't see the mounting uncertainty that was rising within him, or sense the fear that was becoming harder and harder to control.

"I want you to believe this, no matter what happens," Ben Donaley said, placing one hand on Doug's shoulder, "that is, that I love you like my own son and I love Mara as much now as when she was my own daughter-in-law. Nothing or no one will stop me from bringing this whole situation to justice for all concerned—for all the innocent lives lost and ruined by Carlos Antoya and his rivals.

"If it takes my own life to do it—to see it all through—then the worst that can happen is that I will join my son and my wife in heaven, but as the sun rises and sets each day, I will give my all to see justice served."

Doug stood, speechless, next to Ben Donaley. Aside from Mara, Dan's widow, Ellie, and their daughter, Anna, he had no one he could call family in his life. His own father had been a noble man, in the tradition of Ben Donaley, but he had died when both Doug and Dan were young, leaving both men to find their path in life alone.

He was a lucky man to have found someone like Ben Donaley to support him. Mara was the reason. She had brought them together just as destiny had brought her to be his wife. It was as if all the loss, all the pain, all the uncertainty of the past two years was somehow counterbalanced by the deep love he had come to know from those close to him now.

Why couldn't Mara be here right now, safe under Ben Donaley's watch, along with him?

For a moment, his mind flashed back to the day when, as a young boy, he had lost his place on his Little League team because of a broken arm.

"Something good always comes of something bad," he could hear his mother's voice saying as clearly as if it were that day. "No matter how sad you feel, know that one day you will smile again."

Sure enough, the next school year, he had been tagged by the new coach who had watched him play several times, and had gone on to play baseball for his school all the way through high school and then into college—taking his team to victory after victory with his pitching skills.

Instinctively, he knew that this time things would also work out as they were supposed to, when they were supposed to.

Turning to the man who had taken him under his wing, he told Ben, "I give you my word that I'll do all I can to not betray your faith and trust in me."

"I know that, son," Ben answered. "I know."

CHAPTER FORTY-FOUR

Tok

MARA WAS DEFINITELY READY FOR BED BY THE TIME SHE DROVE INTO TOK. Already it was dark and the spring air held a definite chill. Her vehicle's thermometer read 28 degrees.

"You can let the wolf sleep in your room if he don't howl and you don't tell no one," the young desk clerk told her.

"I appreciate that and so does Thor," Mara answered as Thor stood up on his hind legs and licked the clerk on her face.

"I'll give him a piece of my caribou jerky," the girl said.

Thor licked his lips and eagerly swallowed the tasty treat.

"He loves *that*," Mara laughed.

Gathering up her things, she headed to her room with Thor following right behind. The motel was near the edge of town—not that Tok was any kind of booming metropolis by anyone's standards. As she took the last of her things inside, she saw the northern lights swirling overhead. They were intense, like they often were in the spring, and in colors that ranged from green to turquoise with a few strands of pink appearing now and then.

She leaned up against her SUV and watched them. They were mesmerizing. How many people got to see this? The sight of them felt overwhelming, like a rare privilege given only to a few. How wonderful it would be if Doug were here to see this.

She laughed out loud, right there in the parking lot. Had she just wished for Doug? The last time she had been here it had been all about Brad. This time, instead of crying tears of sadness at a man lost, she was longing for togetherness with a man who was in her present—a man who said he loved her as much as she loved him.

She started to dial her cell phone to call him, but stopped before pushing the last two numbers. This time she would not trouble Ben Donaley by asking him to re-route the call so late at night. If she had known that at Ellie's ranch in Palmer Doug was standing outside the bunkhouse at that very moment watching the aurora and thinking the same thing, it would have made her smile.

A wolf howled off in the distance and then another. Thor put his ears back and started to raise his head as if readying to howl back, but instead, he nuzzled up against her leg and quietly followed her inside room 10 of the twelve-room chain that made up the motel. Putting some bottled water in the bowl she always carried for him, she watched as he perked his ears up when the wolves howled again.

"I know you want to talk to them, Thor," she said, stroking Thor's back, "but you're with me now—and Doug—and we're your pack."

Thor put one paw over his nose and nuzzled her again before lying down on the floor. Minutes later, he eagerly chomped down the dog food she had put in another bowl beside his water dish, while she finished arranging the things she would need from her bags.

She took a long, hot shower before getting into bed. Too tired to sleep, she flicked on the TV, amazed that a place this remote had cable TV. The tail end of a news story caught her attention:

> Multiple police agencies, including the Alaska State Troopers are asking for the public's helping finding the location of a person of interest in yesterday's murder of Ethan Shepherd in Butte, Alaska. Officials describe a Hispanic male, 6 feet tall and weighing approximately 180 pounds as a possible suspect in this homicide. The public is being warned that the individual they are seeking is armed and dangerous and may be trying to flee the state. They advise anyone who sees someone fitting this description to notify police immediately. The suspect was last seen driving the small, light blue, late-model sedan belonging to the victim.
>
> This is a breaking news story. Stay tuned to this station for more information as it becomes available to us.

She had already locked the doors to her SUV and to her room, and had already secured the deadbolt, but she pushed the *lock* button on her key fob again just to hear the reassuring honk that said the SUV doors were secured.

When she peeked out the curtains, she saw nothing but her own car out in front of her end of the motel. Four other vehicles sat at the other end of the building. Each of them had a layer of frost already formed on their windshields indicating that the vehicles had been there for a while. For now, everything seemed okay. Still, she hated being alone like this and wondered if a day would come when she would ever get used to it.

Patting the bed with her open hand, she called Thor to her and watched him stretch out on the bed crosswise. With just enough room at the foot to wiggle her own feet under the covers, she went to sleep wishing that she still had the .38 that Karen Steele had loaned her in Juneau. In her head, she could hear Doug's voice repeating the same words he always did when the subject of guns came up.

"You can carry a gun if you want to, but you better be prepared to use it and you better know how to aim it, and mean it if you ever decide to take it out," he had often told her. "And always know that someone can take it away from you and use it against you if you're not careful—but if you want one, then let's take some classes and get you ready."

At this point, she wanted to feel ready, but deep inside she knew that she wasn't, and so she pulled the covers up close and covered her head until she fell asleep.

CHAPTER FORTY-FIVE

Della

Mara sat bolt upright in bed. The alarm clock read 5 a.m. as she heard the doorknob jiggle and then jiggle again. She froze, daring not even to breathe, and carefully laid one hand across Thor's nose, willing him to stop his persistent low growls as he sat poised for action on the bed beside her.

Thor put his chin on the blankets, lowered his ears and stared at the door. The sound of the footsteps moved slowly away before the jiggling of another doorknob further down the line of rooms that made up the strip motel kept her frozen in fear. She took several tiny breaths as she listened. More steps, more distant sounds of doorknob rattling, and then silence.

A woman's scream, a gunshot, the shrill sound of a car alarm, and the squealing of tires pierced the early morning stillness before, once again, there was silence.

Huddled, quivering under the covers, as if the motel bedding would protect her from an assassin's bullet, Mara dared not move. When her heart began to pound against her chest with a force that she feared would kill her, she lifted the blankets off her head and sucked in a deep breath, and then another. It was only 5:15 a.m.—barely fifteen minutes from when she had been awakened.

The wail of distant sirens was becoming louder. Thank God, someone had summoned help. She took another breath, forcing it in so much it hurt. Why were her lungs so tight? Was she having a heart attack? She reached for her pulse. How fast was too fast? She began to pant, pressing her fingers harder against her wrist as she did. She started for the door, but before she could walk the few feet to go outside, she heard the sound of racing vehicles roar by as the sirens faded away in the other direction. Why did she feel so dizzy? She ran to the bed and lay down as she forced herself to breathe slowly and deeply until she was pretty sure she wasn't going to die.

Was that someone moaning? She got up, put her ear to the door, and heard the sound once more. Fear kept her from looking outside, but when she heard the moan again, this time louder, she slowly cracked the door open, leaving the chain lock in place. It was dark outside, with only the yellow light above the motel office door shining down into the blackness.

"Help me…please help me…" a woman cried faintly.

After fumbling to unhook the chain lock, she opened the door to let Thor out. She watched his dark silhouette nervously circle the parking area before hovering over something on the ground near the motel office door. By now, other patrons were coming out of their rooms as Thor ran back to her, whimpering in a way that indicated he wanted her to follow.

Clutching her robe tightly to her, Mara walked slowly out into the parking lot.

"I called 911," someone said.

"So did I," someone else said. "They said the sirens we heard were the police and that the ambulance is coming from farther away. It should be here any time now."

Lying on the ground outside the motel office just beyond the beam of the light was the young clerk who had checked them in last night. She was clutching her left arm under which a pool of blood was beginning to coagulate on the ground.

"Please, help me. Please, help me. Somebody call 911. I've been shot," the young woman pleaded in the thick accent that marked her Alaska Native heritage.

Mara knelt down beside her. The young woman was as white as a sheet, and the wound to her left arm was substantial, with fragments of bone sticking out of the ragged, gaping wound the bullet had left. With nothing else to use, she slid off Thor's collar and used it as a tourniquet, slowing the flow of blood to a trickle, loosening it every few minutes to let whatever blood that could, get to the woman's lower arm, before tightening it once again.

"Do you remember me?" Mara asked her, trying to keep her awake.

The woman's eyes rolled up in her head.

""What's your name?" Mara barked, snapping the woman back to consciousness.

"Dell…De…Dell…a," the woman whispered.

"Listen to me, Della," Mara said firmly, as Della's eyes began to roll upward again. "Della! Open your eyes!"

Somehow she had to make the woman stay awake.

"Open your eyes, Della!"

Della mouthed the word, "Okay," before her eyes fluttered closed again.

A crowd of people had gathered around behind Mara. Someone handed her a blanket, which she draped over Della. Someone else said the ambulance was just turning in.

"We're going to have to move her over to the clinic until the medevac gets here from Anchorage," an arriving state trooper, who said he was trained in trauma rescue stated. "Anybody know what happened here?"

Opening a first aid bag that was larger than most, the trooper removed a large wad of absorbent bandage and pressed it against the wound on Della's arm. Mara flinched right along with Della.

"You can take the tourniquet off now," the trooper told her.

"My dog and I heard something that woke us up about five and then we heard screams, a shot, and more screaming, before I heard a vehicle roar off with screeching tires," Mara told him.

An EMT edged Mara aside and began taking Della's vital signs, after which he carefully placed a splint under her left arm while Thor stayed protectively near Della's head.

"You're gonna need to call back your dog," he snapped at Mara.

"No!" Della cried, "The wolf found me and saved my life."

"C'mere Thor," Mara called.

"This yours?" the medic asked, handing Mara Thor's blood-soaked collar.

Bile rose into Mara's mouth as she took the collar from him, and then she vomited right there in front of everyone—over and over again until she felt she would pass out right there next to Della. Someone helped her back to her room and laid her on her bed, placing a cold washcloth on her forehead. When she woke up later, Thor's clean collar was hanging on the doorknob, and Thor was lying beside her on the floor.

By the time she summoned up the courage to walk back outside, night was descending once again, and there was only a dark spot covered by a dusting of snow where Della had bled on the ground.

All but two of the cars that had been there earlier were gone and the motel office was dark with a *closed* sign hung on the door. A lone security guard sat in his car with the engine running in the shadows of the office.

Nighttime or no nighttime, Mara dialed Ben Donaley and asked him to connect her with Doug.

CHAPTER FORTY-SIX

Border Drama

"WHY DIDN'T YOU TELL ME YOU WERE ON YOUR WAY BACK?" DOUG SNAPPED when Mara told him about the incident at the motel in Tok.

"I could have come to get you," he added, as if those words alone could have prevented her from being near the shooting at the motel.

He stopped talking, barely listening as she tried to explain. It wasn't like him to be this tense and condescending. His words had sounded harsh, even to his own ears. He swallowed hard. Mara was scared and he was, too.

"Look. I'm sorry," he told her, feeling his frustration rise at the sound of her tears. "Just calm down, okay?"

Why was he so antsy? There was no proof that this act of violence was in any way connected to the series of tragedies that had dogged him and his family for two years. This could have been—probably was, even—a totally unrelated act.

On the other hand, what if it wasn't? What if whoever murdered Ethan Shepherd—not *whoever*—what if Carlos Antoya was in Tok? What if he had been the shooter at the motel? For the first time in years, he wanted a cigarette. Pretty weird thought since he hated cigarettes.

What horrible coincidence had placed Mara at the very motel where Della had been shot for her car—especially when he hadn't been there to protect her? Sassy's murder had supposedly been pure coincidence, too. Two strange, terrible coincidences involving violence toward people he loved—three if you counted Dan's murder; this was getting much too "coincidental" to be simple coincidence.

"Doug, are you there?" Mara said through the phone.

"I'm sorry, Mara, I got caught up in my thoughts. I'm just so relieved that you're okay."

He had been wrong to jump on her. There was no way Mara could possibly have known the whole story of why he had been fearful enough to take the tone with her that he had. There he was thinking about cigarettes again. What was it with the blasted cigarettes, anyway? Adding to Mara's fears by telling her about Ethan's murder might be more than she could handle on top of what had just happened, but there was no choice but to explain.

"There was a murder at Sassy's house," he told her. "Ethan Shepherd, you know, the bodyguard and friend of Sassy's daughter, Erin? He was shot as he pushed her out of the way of an attempt on her life."

He heard Mara gasp. She wasn't used to seeing him be so edgy, which only made him edgier.

"I heard something like that just happened in the Butte," she said, "but I had no idea he was with Sassy's daughter."

"I don't want to say anymore over the phone," Doug said, "but I want you to be on the highest alert as you drive this way. Better yet, I want you to stay right there. Do you feel safe there?"

"Yes," Mara answered. "Safe enough. There's been a security guard here ever since the shooting. I've pretty much been staying in my room and when I do go out for food, I take Thor with me and usually go only during the day."

"Stay there," Doug told her. "I'll be there tomorrow, early. I'm going to get a couple of hours sleep and then head out around 3 a.m."

"You should wait until morning. The darkness…the moose…"

"Hold on a second, Doug," she said, "Something's happening on the local news." Lowering the phone to her side, she turned up the volume on the TV.

"They're showing a picture of Tok," she told him. "Just a minute…"

Doug turned on his own TV and listened along with his wife as the reporter spoke:

> Alaska State Troopers report that a man has been found dead at the Eagle, Alaska border crossing. The man has been identified as repairman for the Canadian Border Patrol who had been working on restoring communication links lost during recent storms in the area.
>
> A vehicle fitting the description of the one stolen from a Tok, Alaska Motel yesterday, and being driven by a man fitting the description of wanted fugitive Carlos Antoya, is shown on a security camera at the site breaking through a barricade at the closed border crossing.
>
> Canadian Mounted Police have formed a roadblock just east of the border crossing station where they discovered the body during a routine patrol about two hours ago. The

border station had been expected to open in two days but has now been closed indefinitely.

At this time, officials are urging all travelers to seek alternate routes, as well as to proceed with extreme caution. The suspect is considered to be armed and dangerous, further complicating an already tense situation where numerous washouts in the road have stranded several travelers and left them few options for escape. Alaskan and Canadian officials are working to establish a safe route for stranded travelers and are flying in extra law enforcement teams to secure the area.

It is uncertain at this time what direction the person responsible for this crime took and there is concern that he may have retreated into Alaska in a desperate attempt to elude capture. Alaska State Troopers are working cooperatively with Canadian authorities in an effort to apprehend the suspect, who is also considered to be the person responsible for the attempted murder of a motel clerk in Tok yesterday.

Anyone seeing a vehicle with the make and license number matching the one printed on this screen, below, is urged to contact authorities immediately.

Do not attempt to stop or interfere with the flight of this individual.

Repeat—This person is armed and dangerous. Do not attempt to stop or interfere with the flight of this individual.

Contact authorities immediately if you see or suspect you may have seen someone matching the description given during this bulletin.

This is a breaking news story. We will bring you more information as it becomes available.

Doug could hear the shaking in his wife's voice as she asked him if he had heard all of what she just had.

"Stay inside," he said with steely calm. "I'm on my way."

CHAPTER FORTY-SEVEN

Gift from Mary

Mara bumped awkwardly against the door frame as she and Thor squeezed out of the motel room for Thor's last outing of the night. When she heard something rustle in the shadows near the end of the building about two doors down, she stepped back against the wall of the motel, tightening her grip on the wooden towel rod she had grabbed from the bathroom for protection.

Thor strained at his leash at her reaction, but seemed otherwise unfazed by the sound. Minutes later, a porcupine waddled across the yard in front of the end unit of the motel and moved toward a stand of birch along the edge. She had just loosened her grip on the towel rod when a man's voice startled her into jumping clear off the wooden deck that ran in front of the motel.

"Sorry, Ma'am," the security guard said. "I thought you saw me."

"Oh, thank goodness it's you," she answered, trying to compose herself while the guard gave Thor a piece of moose jerky, just like he had done the last time she saw him.

"He sure loves that moose jerky," The guard laughed. "Got to ration it out to him or I'll lose my whole evening snack."

"Have you heard any more about the person who shot Della?" Mara asked.

"Just about the shootin' of the border guard up in Boundary off the Taylor Highway this afternoon," he answered. "I figure it was our man, though. Sorry son-of-a..."

Mara watched the guard straighten the waistband on his trousers and finger the gun he carried on his belt.

"And Della, how's she doing? Have you heard anything?" she asked him.

"She's okay," the guard answered. "They saved her arm, but she's got some permanent damage to her bicep. Still, her mother told me she can use her hand and that the doctors are sayin' she'll be pretty much back to normal after a couple of months of therapy and a coupla more surgeries."

"It sounds like you know the family well then?" Mara asked.

"Small town, ya know. Della's ma, and me—well, we go back a ways. I've known Della since she was just a newborn baby brought about by her mother's fling with a teenage crush that she thought she loved. Kid left her before Della was born. Yup. Left Mary to raise the baby alone."

The guard reached into his upper front jacket pocket and took out a small trinket of some sort, which he handed to her.

"Mary—Della's mother—Mary wanted me to give this to you in appreciation for the help you gave her daughter."

"By the way, my name's Henry," he said.

Mara examined the trinket as Henry watched her intently.

"It's quite lovely," Mara told him.

"It's a porcupine quill bracelet," Henry said. "Mary said if you don't like the colors, she'll make you a different one, but she said to tell you she liked this one because it reminded her of the northern lights."

"It is absolutely the most beautiful work of art I have ever owned," Mara said, fidgeting with balancing the bracelet between her wrist and her knee so she could close the intricate clasp with her free hand.

When she was done, she held her arm out and admired it. With the white quills accented with iridescent dark blue beads, she could almost imagine a snowy winter's night and the aurora illuminating the landscape below.

"It's gorgeous," she said, holding her arm away from herself to admire it. "I don't know what to say. Please tell Mary how much I like it and how happy I am that Della will be okay."

"Mary also wanted me to give this to you for the wolf," Henry said, handing her a round, beaded medallion, about the size of a quarter.

The medallion was made up of a continuous line of beads that were sewn in a circular fashion onto a piece of hide that Henry said was moose. Somehow, in the intricacy of the beading, Mary had formed the image of a howling wolf's head in the center, using beads that matched those in her bracelet.

"Mary hopes you will put this on the wolf's collar to help him know he is loved by her and her daughter," Henry said.

Mara stooped to attach the medallion to the ring that held Thor's other tags. Thor shook his head and circled about for a few turns before lying back down at Mara's feet.

"Again, I don't know what to say," Mara said.

Words were not enough to thank this woman who had taken the time to create such gifts while her daughter lay in a hospital healing from a violent attack. Most people would have been consumed with anger, or overcome with inertia, but Mary had been thoughtful enough to think of her and Thor.

Suddenly Mara handed Thor's leash to Henry.

"Watch him for me for a moment, Henry. Would you please?" she said, as she went back inside her room. A few minutes later she returned, holding the feather that Joe Michael had given her on the ferry almost two years ago.

"This is one of the most precious things I own," she said. "And like all precious things, its goodness can only be enriched when it is shared."

Henry took the feather from Mara and placed it gently into his inside breast pocket.

"Please tell Mary and Della that this is from me. Tell them that I hope it brings them the same safety from danger that it has brought me. And tell them that I hope it helps them find the same path to freedom from all that stifles their dreams that it has brought to me."

"But if this is so important..." Henry said.

"No. Please, Henry, do as I ask. It is time for me to pass it to the place where it needs to be. Give it to Mary and Della and tell them what I said. I know Mary will understand."

"I'll do it tonight—right after my shift, "Henry told her. "Soon as I get home to my two girls."

Mara smiled.

"They are lucky to have someone like you," she told him, watching as his eyes misted over.

"Not as lucky as me," he said, winking. "You have a safe walk now. I'll be keepin' an eye out."

After alerting Henry to the fact that Doug would be arriving for her sometime during the night, Mara finished her walk with Thor and went to sleep until the sound of Doug's truck pulling in woke her.

CHAPTER FORTY-EIGHT

Passing the Legacy

MARA SNUGGLED AGAINST DOUG'S BACK, WATCHING HIM SLEEP. HAD SHE done the right thing in impulsively giving the feather from Joe Michael to Della? Yes, of course she had. A stranger had given it to her and now she had given it to a stranger—passed on the legacy, or whatever.

The feather had brought her strength through all the turmoil of the past two years. It had been a cherished treasure and a constant presence in her Alaskan life. It wasn't as though she believed in magic or anything. Really, it had been not so much the feather itself, but the kindness of the act of handing it to her that had changed her life so powerfully—at least that is what she would always believe.

Rubbing Doug's back gently to quiet his restless sleep, she remembered the day Joe Michael had given the feather to her, and the mysterious words he had spoken as she stood on the car deck of the Alaska State ferry *Malaspina*.

Your present is the future of your past.

All who come here seek the future of their past.

You will need this to protect your future from your past.

Little had she known at that moment that her past would indeed come back to haunt her in the most powerful way one could imagine, yet here she was nearly two years later, lying safely next to the man she loved more than life itself. She felt secure, even in the face of the danger that had reappeared in her life—secure, and stronger.

And there had been Joe Michael's powerful passing, followed by his un-believable return. His confession that he had faked his own death had done nothing to diminish the sacrifice he had made for her own life. If anything, it had cemented her trust in him—a trust felt intensely, but yet not explainable by any rational means.

First Joe, then Sal Kindle. Wonderful Sal. Sal, who just as Joe had done, had entered her life when least expected. Sal—there to take her in and shield her from danger not just once, but three times already now. Sal, who had unbelievably turned out to be the new love of none other than Joe Michael, giving her not one, but two guardian angels, it seemed.

Just as Joe, then Sal, had come to her, she would try to give strength to Della—a person who, like she had been to both Joe and Sal, was a stranger and an innocent victim of circumstances—circumstances that might even be linked to Mara's own past. Passing the feather to Della felt right. Surely, she did not feel diminished in the giving, rather, it seemed to have brought a new strength to her soul.

Goodness could overcome evil. Joe had taught her that. She would share her own strength with Della now, just as Joe and Sal had done for her. It was time for her to let go of her own frailties and help someone else become strong. Someday, when she was stronger, Della would do the same. Her mother already had, in giving her the quill bracelet and giving Thor the medallion.

Glancing down at the quill bracelet that Mary had made for her in Della's name, Mara smiled. The neutral white of the porcupine quill had depth and substance—like ivory. She fingered the iridescent dark blue beads. Just as they had when she first saw the bracelet, they spoke to her again of the northern lights and the gift of awareness wrought on all who viewed them.

She reached down and fingered the matching medallion on Thor's collar, knowing that Thor was part of the legacy begun by Joe Michael, and perhaps others before him of which she was not aware.

Stronger together than alone against those who sought to do others harm, bit by bit the feathers and quill bracelets and medallions gifted from the hearts of the good would unite the gentle souls of the world against the forces of those who sought to do them harm.

Doug stirred in his sleep and reached for her. She let him tuck her arm under his as she fell asleep beside him. Somewhere outside the safe haven of the motel room in Tok, Alaska, a murderer or murderers lurked in the shadows, but for now, she, Doug and Thor were safe in their room. As she drifted into sleep beside her husband, somewhere in a hospital in Anchorage Mary was handing Della the feather sent to give her the strength to be free of harm.

Miles away, in yet another direction, Joe Michael smiled, somehow aware that his legacy had found new life. She wasn't sure if it was a dream, but she saw his smiling face and felt his warm approval.

CHAPTER FORTY-NINE

The Ditch

THE MESSAGE INTERCEPTED BY BEN DONALEY DISTURBED HIM. IT WAS NOT unusual for him to pick up communications between law enforcement agencies. It was part of the security clearance he held and more importantly, an inherent part of the work he did. This message, though, confirmed that both Doug and Mara could be in imminent danger.

He listened to an Alaskan police official talk to Canadian Mounties.

> We are advised that the suspect in the murder of Ethan Shepherd and the attempted murder of Della Johnson, as well as the murder of a Canadian custom's agent may be responsible for the attempted theft of an airplane south of Eagle, Alaska.

> The owner of the plane reports that he fired three shots at a fleeing person fitting the description of Carlos Antoya. He further reports that gunfire was returned and that the suspect fled the scene in a stolen white jeep taken from one of the campers stranded by flooding in the area.

> The suspect is considered armed and extremely dangerous and was last seen attempting to cross a washed-out section of the Taylor Highway by driving around barricades and onto a temporary shoulder constructed for rescue purposes.

> He was later reported to have successfully bypassed three other roadblocks and was last seen heading south toward Tetlin.

> We are dispatching troopers from Valdez and Fairbanks to Tok and have advised local police and EMS officials to be on the lookout for the vehicle described above. We are also dispatching a helicopter from Fairbanks to the Tok area. All Canadian border crossings will be secured with…

Ben didn't bother to listen to the rest of the transmission. Doug had gone to Tok to pick up Mara. Why wasn't he answering his phone? Why hadn't he called to report his whereabouts?

He paced inside the hangar for several minutes trying to gather his thoughts. Doug had probably turned it off in order to get some undisturbed sleep after the long drive. That would be the best-case scenario. In any event, he would have some stern words for Doug when he did finally manage to reach him and tell him that his security and that of Mara required that the phone be left on.

Doug's gray Chevy half ton rocked precariously on two tires as it threatened to roll onto its side in the ditch. He heard Thor yelp as he was thrown against the sides of his crate. Luckily, he had secured the cage with straps so it couldn't fly out of the truck bed. A glance at Mara showed that she was all right and he reached over and gave her arm a brief rub. Lucky thing they were both wearing their seatbelts.

The two had just left Glennallen after deciding to leave Mara's SUV with Henry until Doug could fly back to pick it up in a few days. No sooner had they reached the edge of town than they had been driven into the ditch by a mud-covered white jeep that Doug estimated was going at least 100 miles per hour.

"Even if we roll we'll all be okay," he shouted above the creaking sounds of the truck as it rocked from side to side until finally coming to a standstill at about a thirty-degree angle with the driver's side down.

After turning the key to cut the engine, he tried to open his door, but he could only get it open a few inches before it became mired in the muck of the ditch.

"Can you push your door open?" he said to Mara.

He watched her try, but she was not strong enough to push it against the gravity that was holding it down. He slid the rear cab window open, undid his seatbelt, braced his foot against the dashboard, and managed to crawl out into the truck bed. He unlatched Thor's cage and ran his hands over the dog's coat to see if there were any outstanding injuries. Thor, although nervous, seemed all right.

After crawling over the tailgate, he jumped across to the upside of the ditch where he landed on both hands and his knees before regaining his balance enough to move sideways toward the front of the vehicle. After several tries, he found that he was not strong enough to get Mara's door open either.

"Turn the ignition key and lower your window," he told her.

"You're gonna have to crawl out through your window, Mara. There's no other way out."

Mara did as Doug instructed, lying on her belly on her seat and easing herself feet first out the open window. With one final push-off, she slid down the outside of the truck, landing on a tuft of grass that kept her from sinking into the mucky ditch. Holding onto the door handle with one hand, she stretched to reach Doug's outstretched hand with her other. With one big pull, she made it over to the bank and into Doug's arms. Minutes later, they sat on the side of the ditch trying to size up the mess they were in.

Doug's phone rang again.

"Hello—" he began, before the voice at the other end cut him off.

"Doug! I don't know why the blazes you decided to turn your danged phone off right now," Ben Donaley barked with uncustomary irritation, "but now that I got your attention, I need to warn you that Carlos Antoya may be heading your way in a stolen white jeep. In view of all that's been going on, I want to warn you to avoid him at all costs. Is Mara with you?"

"She's right here," Doug answered.

"You need to get the both of you back to Palmer ASAP," Ben Donaley said.

"Gonna be kinda hard to do," Doug said dryly. "A white jeep just ran us into the ditch just outside of Glennallen and we're sittin' here on the shoulder of the road after just workin' our tails off to get out of it in one piece."

"S—!" Doug thought he heard an expletive from Ben's end of the phone. "You two all right?"

"We're not hurt," Doug answered. "Thor's with us and he's okay, too, but I don't think I'm gonna be able to get my truck out of this ditch without some serious help."

"You got your pistol?" Ben asked Doug.

"Yup," Doug answered.

"Stay there with your truck then, and I'll get the troopers to get you some help. It goes without sayin' that they're gonna want a description of what you saw and anything you can tell 'em about what happened."

"Yeah. Okay," Doug answered.

"S—!" came the expletive again. "Just stay safe, doggone it, Doug—and keep your danged phone on."

CHAPTER FIFTY

Santiago

Doug flagged down a passing motorist who agreed to give him and Mara a ride to Glennallen. From there they hitched another ride with a trucker who dropped them off in Tok, where they picked up Mara's SUV.

"Nice folks out this way," Doug told his wife. "Luckily no one asked too many questions."

"But what about Ben and the troopers?" Mara asked him.

"We can't wait for them," Doug snapped. "Let's go."

Doug's sharp tone frightened her.

"Our life depends on it, Mara. Just stay calm and I'll get us to a safe place."

Mara trusted her husband. He had always protected her. As soon as she let Thor in the back of her SUV, she got in the passenger side and sat quietly as Doug drove back to Glennallen and then headed south to Valdez.

"We have to make the ferry," he told her, finally breaking the long silence that had marked the drive so far. "I checked the schedule in Glennallen and the *Chenega* is leaving for Whittiier a little after four p.m. today."

It was then that she realized they had been up all night. It was now 9 a.m. and suddenly she couldn't stay awake any longer.

When she woke up from her nap, she and Doug were alongside the Lowe River in Keystone Canyon outside Valdez. The fog was so dense that they could barely see the road, and she could feel the spray from the waterfalls that fell from hundreds of feet on each side of the road. Somehow Doug managed to find the turnout and pulled in beside the Horseshoe Falls.

A pickup truck was stopped ahead of them at the opposite end of the long turnout with its engine running, but its lights turned out, and she could see the faint silhouette of a second truck parked on the opposite side of the road.

"Get out!" Doug whispered, as the sound of an approaching vehicle broke through the roar of the raging river and the many waterfalls around them.

Pushing his door open, he got out of the SUV, forgetting to grab the keys from the ignition in his haste. Ducking low, he worked his way around to her side, while she signaled Thor to jump over the seat and follow them. Carefully, she closed the door, pressing herself against it to muffle the click of the latch.

Doug placed his arm around her waist as they scurried to the edge of the pullout to a narrow trail beside the waterfall. Grabbing her hand, he led her up the stony pathway to a place behind the falls where they pulled Thor close to them, crouched there, and waited.

Mara felt Thor tense as someone spoke. Just as she had in Tok, she placed the flat of her hand over his nose, silently telling him not to bark. She felt him relax, even as she saw his ears perk up.

"Santiago. How nice to see you."

The words seemed to come from near their SUV and were those of a man speaking sarcastically in broken English.

"Carlos," another man, who sounded older and tired, replied. "I've come to urge you to turn yourself in."

"You followed me to the end of the earth on this one-way road to nowhere to urge me to turn myself in?" Carlos sneered before coughing and spitting loudly.

Doug and Mara hunkered down, pulling Thor more closely to them as they heard a click that sounded like a bullet moving into the chamber of a gun. "Must've taken some work to find me." Carlos coughed and spat again.

"It's not too late, son. Your mother would have wanted better for you."

"Don't speak of my mother!" Carlos hissed. "You should have never allowed them to let her die to save my wretched birth, old man."

"Son, listen to me," Santiago said softly. "It was God's will that you would live and your mother would not—"

"Believe what you will, old man! You fool! You cursed, stupid fool!" Carlos yelled.

"Put the gun down, son," Santiago answered. "Your brother is a priest. He can talk to you about this. Help you…"

Carlos said nothing. Only the sound of his pacing footsteps broke the quiet, before even that sound stopped, leaving a feeling of eerie calm.

"Son—" Santiago began before his words were abruptly interrupted by Carlos' venomous curse.

"Go to the heaven you want to believe exists, old fool. I'll see you in hell."

The sounds of a single shot and a loud moan pierced the air, and then sickening silence.

From their place behind the waterfall, Doug and Mara watched as a shadowy figure ran through the fog, jumped into Mara's SUV, and roared off, leaving them trembling, and Thor bolting from them before returning to huddle at their side.

CHAPTER FIFTY-ONE

Rescue

"GET IN," A WOMAN CALLED THROUGH THE OPEN WINDOW OF AN OLD beater truck.

Doug tightened his grip on Mara's waist and reached for his revolver with his free hand.

"Time's a wastin'," the woman in the truck insisted. "I need to get ya outta here before the cops get here."

Mara knew that voice.

"Sal?"

"Who the hangin' blazes else is constantly rescuin' ya, Jane? Now ya gonna tell yer man to listen up and get in my truck or ya gonna stand there and deal with the cops—'cause I'm guessin' they're gonna have a lotta questions about that dead man named Santiago I just saw drop at the hand of his own son over there."

"Come on, Doug," Mara said, pulling him toward Sal's truck.

Doug told Thor to get up in the truck bed and then climbed into the cab after Mara. As they sped off, Sal explained that it would be at least two hours before officials could reach the site from the north—that is, unless someone got word to the police in Valdez, in which case it would be a lot sooner.

"Lie down, Thor. Stay!" Doug hollered to the nervous animal out the open window.

"How'd you find me…us?" Mara asked Sal.

"Joe sent me," Sal answered. "He was comin' to Tok, but got caught up in the flooding outside Eagle last week. He heard about the murder and the attempted murder and the fugitive on the run. When he got to Tok, he talked to Della."

"That's weird," Mara interjected.

"Not really, Jane," Sal answered. "Della's Joe's sister-in-law's daughter—niece to his dead wife. Della grew up playin' with Joe's kids. After the fire, well, she was all that was lefta those family years, and so he always makes a point to visit her when he's passin' through."

"Unbelievable," Mara whispered.

"Ain't nothin' on this here earth that's unbelievable, Jane," Sal answered. "Like the sayin' goes, we're all connected."

Mara sat between Sal and Doug as the old beater truck bounced down the road toward Valdez. She was deep in thought when Sal made a sudden swerve. Within seconds, Thor was standing with his feet on the rail of the truck bed as a large black bear darted across the road and scampered into the woods.

"Down, Thor," Doug said. "Just a bear."

Thor paced in the truck bed for a minute and then lay back down.

"Anyway," Sal continued, "Della told Joe about the shootin' and how she heard you two had got run off the road outta Glennallen. She said the security guard at the motel saw you two peel off in Jane's SUV in the middle of the night and figured there was trouble. Since I was down in Glennallen vistin' some friends on my own way to meet Joe in Valdez, he told me to watch fer ya and bring ya down so's you kin catch the ferry tonight."

"Unbelievable," Mara said, repeating the only word that came to mind.

"Thought we discussed that already," Sal said wryly as a police car sped past them in the opposite direction with lights swirling and sirens blasting.

"Joe said to tell ya both to git directly on the ferry once I git you to the terminal and that someone ya know is gonna be waitin' there for ya. He said for ya both not to worry 'cause yer gonna be safe in the end—not that the ride along the way to bein' okay ain't gonna be bumpy, though."

Mara squeezed Doug's hand and he squeezed hers back.

"I can' t thank you enough, Sal. Once again you and Joe have been there for me and now for my husband, too. Some day I hope to repay you…"

"That ain't gonna be necessary, Jane," Sal interrupted.

"I want ya to keep this fer a while," she said, handing a pistol to Mara.

"But Doug has a gun," Mara answered.

"Take it, Jane," Sal insisted. "Might help ya ta understand why if I tell ya that the dead man back at the turnout knows some of the same folks that's been helpin' the two of ya all along."

"But I don't know anybody named Santiago…"

Doug nudged her and nodded an okay for her to take the gun. Taking it from Sal, she laid it on her lap.

"No reason ya woulda," Sal answered. "I'll let the others that's been lookin' out fer ya explain. Damn shame, though. Damn shame."

Sal let her voice trail off before adding, "Damn shame he raised a sorry piece a-work like Carlos Antoya after losin' his wife in childbirth to save the pathetic loser. Makes ya wonder, don't it?"

"Wonder?" Mara asked.

"Well, ya got someone like my Joe who loved his family to bits and lost 'em all, and then ya gets a sorry loser like Carlos who don't even 'preciate the life his father gave him. Don't make no sense of fairness at all—the losers livin' and the good folks dyin'…"

Sal stopped her truck in front of the ferry terminal and hurried them out.

"Git movin'—both of ya and yer wolf, too. Ain't gonna be long before things start heatin' up again."

Doug and Mara stood in front of the terminal as Sal and her truck disappeared into the dense fog.

"You got yourself one heck of a friend, Jane," Doug said wryly, in a weak attempt to lighten the mood.

The truth was, no matter what name Sal called his wife, there was nothing funny about the way she had come to her rescue too many times for any of the encounters to just have been coincidence.

"Let's get on board like Sal said," Doug said.

Whoever Sal was, she had taken Mara under her wing more than once and for that he was grateful. Putting his arm around Mara's shoulders he called, "C'mon Thor," as he led his wife and his dog up the gangway, stopping only long enough to put Thor into the crate had been left for the animal on the car deck. Wasn't that like Joe to think of everything?

CHAPTER FIFTY-TWO

What!

"WHAT DO YOU MEAN YOU'RE ON THE FERRY?" BEN DONALEY YELLED INTO Doug's phone.

"Daddy...Ben...they're with me," Karen Steele said, grabbing the phone from Doug.

"Beth?" Mara exclaimed.

"I told you never to call me that," Karen Steele said, putting her hand over the phone.

"Don't worry, this is my husband, Doug, and he knows everything I know," Mara replied.

Karen Steele scowled at Mara and continued talking.

"Don't worry, Ben, I'll take care of them," she told Ben Donaley before hanging up.

"By the way, Ellie said she's worried sick about both of you," Karen said.

"Ellie?" Mara exclaimed.

"She's there with Ben. They're a couple now," Karen said, momentarily reverting to the familiar.

"I know you probably didn't know. No one did. Ben told me himself last week when I saw them holding hands in a restaurant in Palmer."

"Ben? Ellie? Together?" Mara said, dumbfounded. She looked at Doug, who looked equally shocked.

It wasn't the age gap of 15 years that was so shocking; it was more about who Ben was and who Ellie was in relation to their lives that caught them completely off guard.

"They seem happy," Karen said. "I think it's serious between them and Ben is so cute with Anna. Ben said she calls him Mr. Ben. But that's not the only news I have right now, or even the most important news..."

"More news?" Mara asked, tightening her grip on Doug's arm and wondering what actually *could* shock her anymore.

"Santiago Antoya was an IPA agent," Karen said, watching as Doug and Mara exchanged glances.

"Not only that, but he and Ben were partners in the IPA back when Brad was still alive. When Brad was killed, Santiago was one of the first to step in, regularly putting in extra time to try to find the person who had led A.C. to kill Brad. It was during that time that he first became aware that his own son, Carlos, was the drug cartel henchman known as Cookie."

"Cookie?" Mara said as she raised one eyebrow and glanced at Doug.

"I guess he likes cookies...I don't know," Karen said wryly.

"The point is, we are dealing with a man here who has not only killed at least two other people, but has even taken the life of his own father. There is no doubt in my mind," Karen Steele continued, "that Ben Donaley, Ellie, Anna, Erin and even Sarah and Ken are in imminent danger. This heavy fog that's rolling in will stop Carlos from flying out of here and the fact that local police just reported finding your SUV up on blocks with all the wheels removed about five miles out of town tells me that Carlos has no plans to drive out of here either—at least not in your rig.

"Matter of fact, police report that a Latino male fitting Carlos' description was trying to unload tires and rims from an SUV in shops around town. The question is, who is his accomplice and where is Carlos Antoya right now? My guess is that he is on the ferry," Karen continued before anyone could get a word in. "On this very ferry that we are on, and more than likely, trying to get to Palmer."

"Then we're out of here," Doug said, taking Mara by the elbow and starting to walk away.

"You're not going anywhere," Karen Steele said.

"You gonna try to stop us," he said, looking down at her petite frame.

Thrusting her badge in his face, Karen Steele said, "I'm placing you under arrest—both of you."

"Arrest?" Doug laughed, pulling away from the grasp she had on his arm.

"I've got to do something to keep you here," Karen said, grabbing Doug's arm again.

"You're under arrest for leaving the scene of an accident and as a person of interest in the death of Santiago Antoya."

Karen Steele nodded at the agent who had accompanied her onto the ferry, signaling him to handcuff Mara and Doug who both stood open-mouthed in disbelief.

"Run, Mara!" Doug suddenly shouted, sprinting away from the agent who was attempting to cuff him. "Run!"

At that moment, Thor sprung from the cage near where they had been standing and tackled Karen Steele, pushing her to the ground and leaving the other agent to try to assist her. Taking off after his owners, Thor ran with them down the gangway and into the foggy streets of Valdez. Behind them, Karen Steele's fellow agent raised his gun, but felt his arm forced down by his partner.

CHAPTER FIFTY-THREE

Escape

"HELL'S AFIRE, ALREADY, JANE, IF YER NOT IN TROUBLE QUICKER 'N EVEN I predicted you'd be."

Mara felt someone place a hand on her elbow and quickly recognized Sal despite fog so thick it was hard to even see a person standing right next to you.

"My truck's right there," Sal said, pointing into the fog.

Thrusting the keys into Doug's hand, she added, "It'll git ya to Copper Center. Turn into the fish camp there at the Tazlina River and ask fer Minty— that's my second cousin once removed. Minty'll git ya inta somethin' the cops won't be lookin' for and from there you kin head inta Palmer…"

Mara pulled her arm away, causing Sal to hesitate before continuing. "I ain't dumb, Jane. I know dang well you and the Mr. here are tryin' ta git back ta yer people in Palmer. Gol darned, if I'd a-known Joe had taken on someone as scared ta take a helpin' hand as yerself, I don't know that I'd ever a-told him *I do* last week at the courthouse."

"You and Joe got married?" Mara said, surprised.

"Yeah, we got hitched fer danged sure, Jane, and so that makes you my responsibility now, too. Now git yer man and the both of ya git yer behinds on outta here and do like I said so's I kin git back to enjoyin' my honeymoon already."

Mara smiled in spite of the drama unfolding around her. Without warning, she wrapped her arms around Sal and hugged her tightly, kissing her lightly on the cheek. Even in the dense fog, she could see a coat of fresh pink nail polish on Sal's fingernails, as she held both of her hands and kissed each of them, too.

"Thank you," Mara said simply. "Both of you."

Finally Doug spoke, thanking Sal, too, before taking Mara by the hand and moving through the fog to Sal's old truck. He felt Thor nuzzle in between them and opened the door to let the animal get in. Once all three of them were inside, he started up Sal's truck and gave the engine a couple of revs before moving back onto the highway.

Only a few other vehicles were on the road, and the fog worsened the closer they got to the waterfalls through which the highway passed north through Keystone Canyon. When they saw the shadowy splotches of red and blue lights in the mist, they both tensed, but they passed the group of patrol cars in the wide turnout to the left next to Horsetail Falls without incident. Maybe it was the security of Sal's old, familiar truck, but none of the several men working around an object on the ground seemed to be concerned with them passing by. One of them even waved them through.

For a short while, they drove above the fog over Thompson Pass, and from there on, they encountered it only in patchy stretches of lowlands along the rivers that wound through the area.

They stopped for a hamburger at an old lodge, where they let Thor run off some of the energy he had pent up from being confined for so long lately. By the time they reached Copper Center, it was early evening and Minty was just closing up the shop where he repaired engines and sold fishing gear—depending on the season.

With few words exchanged, they left Sal's truck with Minty and accepted the keys to yet another old beater—this one an old Ford the faded color of the rust-colored lichens that grew in the cracks of area rocks.

Doug nodded appreciation as Minty spat his chew on the ground and wiped the back of his sleeve across his mouth as he waved them off. "Tank's full," he called as they sputtered off.

When they looked back, only the dust cloud from the gravel incline that led out of Minty's parking area was visible. By the time they reached Glennallen, Thor had settled into a nap on the front seat, pushing Mara tightly against the door upon which she rested her own tired head.

With both his wife and his dog sound asleep beside him, Doug fought to stay awake as he drove through the wide spot in the road known as Mendeltna. Good that they should rest now, but for him rest would be for later—once the trouble ahead had been met and put aside forever. At least he hoped this time it would be forever, because he had had about all any one man could take.

CHAPTER FIFTY-FOUR

High Stakes

ERIN DE LA CORTE'S SCREAM PEELED THROUGH THE FINGERS OF THE HAND that tried to muffle her voice. Whoever had pulled her down from the horse she had been attempting to mount reeked of stale cigarettes and old booze as he held her tightly against him so that she couldn't get a look at his face.

"Not so rough, D.J.," Carlos said softly. "She is the woman I love more than all the rest."

"Yeah, sure. Sorry, Cookie," D.J. replied, letting go of his grasp on Erin.

Carlos Antoya pushed D.J. against a stall and shoved a pistol under his chin. "Never call me Cookie in public again or you'll be nothing more than a bloodstain on this fine stable here, my friend."

"Yeah, sure, Carlos," D.J. muttered.

Erin stood trembling, watching the scene before her until Carlos put his arms around her, pulled her close, and kissed her firmly.

"Why so tense, my love," Carlos said in that sickly-sweet tone that Erin knew only too well.

"Just surprised to see you, Carlos," she said coolly. "Perhaps your wife didn't tell you that I left you once I found out you were married."

"Ah, Imelda, God rest her soul. Have you not heard? I'm a grieving widower now. The speeding car—they never caught them…"Carlos said, turning his back on Erin as he spoke.

Erin froze and tried to recover enough composure to face what she now knew would be the fight of her life.

"I didn't know, Carlos. I'm so sorry," Erin said.

"You never told me you were Amanda Carlson's daughter," Carlos said, stroking her hair.

"I never knew I was until right before she died," Erin replied. "Angus and Monica are the only parents I ever knew."

"But somehow you found her, my love, did you not," Carlos said, his voice no more than a low growl.

"She found me. Wrote to me. Wanted to meet me—so I asked my mother how she felt about it and she gave me her blessing. I was so happy she found me," Erin said, her eyes welling with tears, "and so sorry to lose her."

"Ah, such sentiment. You are just as I knew you, Erin, all soft and caring inside and—well—quite the opposite of me."

Erin could see Carlos furrow his brow. It was unusual for him to talk about his feelings, and just as quickly as he had opened the door to his emotions, he slammed it shut again.

"Are you sure you did not come just for the money, Erin darling?" he said coldly.

"Money?" Erin asked him.

"It's long past the time to play dumb with me, love," Carlos sneered, grasping Erin's chin between his thumb and forefinger before pushing her away.

"It's here, all right," D.J. interjected. "My father told me it was."

"Your father?" Erin asked.

"Adam Carlson," D.J. shot back. "I'm A.C.'s son. Just call me cousin."

"I knew my mother had a brother," Erin said quietly. "She talked of him often, of how she loved him—Adam."

"That's right. Adam Carlson—A.C.," D.J. told her.

"I never met or spoke to him though," Erin said.

"I'm sorry, cousin, but I find that just almost impossible to believe. Now where's the money!" D.J. barked.

"I don't know anything about any money," Erin answered.

"You may have heard by now that I'm not such a nice guy," Carlos interrupted.

"That's right. He's killed better people than you," D.J. snapped. "Women are a dime a dozen to men like Carlos Antoya."

"Shut up, D.J.," Carlos said.

"We'll talk about it in the morning, Erin. For now, well, it's been a long time since we were together and the night is still young."

Erin did not resist going into her mother's house with Carlos. She knew it would be of no use. What she did do was to push 911 on her cell phone and drop it into the bushes outside the front door. Somehow, she now had to think of a plan of escape for when Carlos and D.J. would hear the approaching sirens.

CHAPTER FIFTY-FIVE

Heating up

THE MINUTE THE 911 CALL CAME IN FROM ERIN'S ADDRESS BEN DONALEY WAS alerted as part of a cooperative effort with Alaska law enforcement agencies. When Ken Tandry called to reassure him no lights or sirens would be used by law enforcement when responding to the call made by Erin, it was welcome relief.

"I don't feel good about this, Ben," Tandry said.

"That's not the worst of it," Ben Donaley replied. "Karen Steele just alerted me that Doug and Mara broke free from her as she was trying to arrest them just to keep them safe. She thinks they had some help in finding a way out of Valdez and they may be on their way to Palmer right now."

"Do you think they'd have any reason to go to Erin's?" Tandry asked.

"Not necessarily," Ben answered, "but they might try to go to your place or here to Ellie's—which I think is the most logical choice. If Carlos Antoya is holding Erin hostage, then the situation could deteriorate rapidly."

Ben hesitated for a moment before continuing, "Ken, my dau…Agent Karen Steele told me that Carlos murdered his own father in Valdez yesterday."

Ben's voice choked with emotion. "Santiago Antoya was not just another agent of the IPA, he was my friend."

"I don't mean to sound insensitive, Ben, but how can you be sure it was Carlos who killed him?" Tandry asked.

"Santiago was an experienced agent. He was known to carry a voice recorder, and when he was in suspicious circumstances, to turn it on. This time was no exception. We have a recording of the entire conversation between Santiago and Carlos, including name and location identification, as well as other facts linking the two as father and son."

The next piece of information was the hardest for Ben Donaley to relay. "I heard the recording myself," he said. "Agent Steele played it for me. It included the gunshot and the last moans of my good friend, Santiago."

Ben Donaley stopped talking for a few minutes before he spoke again. "You know, Ken, I've been in this business a long time. I've seen agents come and agents go. Sometimes I've enjoyed the success of capturing some of the really bad guys, just as I've occasionally been able to help exonerate those who are innocent. But…" Ben paused again before continuing, "But I've lost my son and my wife to this business, and I've seen my friends lose their loved ones, too. Now I've lost a good friend and one of the most loyal and respected agents in the business."

"I know it's got to be hard," Tandry said weakly, unsure of what he actually could say in the way of comfort at a time like this.

"And now my son's wife and her new husband are in danger along with the lives of so many other good people," Ben said. "I just don't know if I have the stomach for this anymore."

This time Tandry said nothing.

"Don't worry, I'll see it through. Somehow I always get my second wind right when I need it. When it's over, though, I intend to marry Ellie—that is, if she'll have an old codger like me for a husband. I want to help her raise Anna, and take care of the ranch and just live a normal life for the future—know what I mean?"

"I know what you mean," Tandry answered. He had felt much the same way right before marrying Sarah. That their new baby would be born soon was all that mattered anymore. Soon he, too, would retire, and become the family man he wanted to be.

Tandry wanted to talk more, to caution Ben not to let his guard down and to bring him back from the sentimental mind-set that he knew would work against his police instincts, but the sound of the door opening stopped him.

"They're here, Ben," he said into the phone. "Doug and Mara just walked in."

"I'll be right up," Ben answered.

"You stay put, Ben," Tandry said with uncharacteristic firmness. "As soon as Ellie and Anna get home, get them out of there to someplace safe and then come back to Ellie's ranch. I don't want to overrule you, Ben, but I've danced this dance before and I can almost guarantee you that Carlos Antoya and whoever his accomplice is will be in your backyard before the day is through."

Ben heard the sound of Ellie pulling up in her car and heard the door slam as young Anna ran toward him.

"Mr. Ben, Mr. Ben, guess what Momma and I bought in Palmer today?"

Scooping Anna into his arms, Ben said to Tandry, "I'll take your advice starting right now, and I'll call you as soon as I am headed back."

"Ellie, pack a few clothes for you and Anna and get back in the car," Ben called. "I'll explain along the way."

CHAPTER FIFTY-SIX

It's Time

"Mara!" Sarah gasped. "You're so thin."

Mara dropped her pack on the floor and met Sarah midway across her living room.

"I can barely get my arms around you," Mara told her, reaching down to gently touch her friend's pregnant belly.

"I know," Sarah said looking down and rubbing her belly herself. "I think it's going to be soon. See how much the baby has dropped?"

Mara stepped back and looked at her friend. Sarah did indeed look like she would give birth soon. It was hard to believe she was already within two weeks of her due date—almost as hard as it was to believe that she had been on the run for almost the entire length of her friend's pregnancy. Sitting down beside Sarah on the sofa, she listened to every detail of the past several months, and then she told Sarah her own story about life on the run.

While Sarah and Mara talked, Ken Tandry took Doug aside.

"There's trouble at Sassy's place," Ken said. "Ben Donaley is moving Ellie and Anna to a safe place right now, and then he's going to meet up with me back at Ellie's ranch."

"Why there?" Doug asked, suddenly feeling the hair on the back of his neck stand up.

Ken Tandry explained. Police had received a 911 call from Erin's cell phone. For several reasons, including the phone call, Ben Donaley had said he expected Carlos Antoya would be turning up at Ellie's looking for both him and Ellie—possibly with Erin De la Corte as a hostage.

"At least, we hope taking Erin as a hostage is the worst thing that happens to her. We have reason to believe that Carlos thinks you or Ellie know something about the money A.C. apparently hid somewhere on Sassy's property."

"Money?" Doug said.

"Drug money A.C. allegedly stole from the South American cartel, and which he owed to Carlos and his thugs in his work as a double agent for Carlos' faction of the Mexican cartel. We also think his finding Erin living at Sassy's place was pure coincidence—almost as a big a coincidence as finding out that she is Sassy's daughter.

"It goes without saying that none of this bodes well for Erin's fate at the hands of Carlos Antoya. To say he is paranoid and desperate is an understatement. The only question is, will the fact that he still carries a torch for her be enough to spare her his wrath? Let's face it, the guy's already killed his father and his wife in cold blood. Doesn't sound like there's much that would stop him from doing the same to Erin, you, Ellie, or anyone else."

Doug cringed hearing Tandry's words and for a moment no one said anything.

Then the totally unexpected happened; Sarah's water broke.

"I need to get to the hospital," Sarah said calmly, as first Mara, and then Ken and Doug scrambled to her side.

"You're gonna have to handle this without me, Doug," Tandry said, his voice shaking with controlled calm as he punched in a phone number on his cell phone.

"Get a SWAT team up to Amanda Carlson's old place in the Butte and get another one on standby for Ellie William's place on Knik River Road," he barked into the phone. "Tell Jones he's in charge. I got an emergency of my own and Sarah and I are on our way down to the hospital in Palmer."

Leaving the person on the other end no time to respond, Ken Tandry shoved his phone into his pocket. Sweat poured from his brow as he took Sarah by one arm while he and Mara walked her to the car.

Doug Williams stood in the doorway alone and feeling helpless, before regaining his composure and stepping back inside. As soon as he cleaned up the mess left on the floor, he would call Thor inside and try to get hold of Ben Donaley.

Meanwhile, Sarah's labor pains had begun in earnest. With Mara stroking her friend's hair to calm her, Ken drove to the hospital as if he were on an official police chase.

By the time they arrived at the emergency room door, Sarah's contractions were five minutes apart.

"It's moving along pretty fast for a primeip," Mara heard one nurse tell another. "Better get her doctor on the line and call for some in-house support from the OB resident. Looks like this baby isn't gonna let anything stand in the way of his arrival."

CHAPTER FIFTY-SEVEN

Feet to the Fire

"ERIN, MY LOVE," CARLOS SAID AS HE PULLED A FEW ITEMS OUT OF HER lingerie drawer. "I forgot how sexy you look in purple."

"Put this on," he ordered, throwing the camisole at the shaking woman who sat on the bed, "while you remember where you hid A.C.'s bank book. Surely it was here with his loving sister's belongings, and is now in the safe possession of her loving illegitimate daughter."

Carlos hardened tone and saccharine voice frightened Erin.

"There is no bank book, Carlos, I swear," Erin said, no longer able to hold back her tears.

"Now, now, my sweet," Carlos said, stroking her cheek. "Let's not talk about that right now."

Fighting the urge to recoil at his touch, Erin forced her emotions off as Carlos raped her. When he was done, she let him sleep while she washed every scent of him she could from her body, vomiting in the shower so he wouldn't hear. When she heard him stir, she quickly lay down again and feigned sleep. Her life depended on his not suspecting she might run. Praying that help would arrive soon, she wondered if her 911 call had gone through, and why it was taking so long for help to arrive.

"The baby came in less than two hours," Mara told Doug over the phone, "But it looks like he's all right."

"Yes, it's a boy," she said in answer to his questions. "seven pounds four ounces…yes, healthy…she's fine, too…Ken's a wreck."

Doug kept his voice upbeat, trying to conceal his fear. Would Carlos and his accomplice even be able to find Ken and Sarah's place even if they thought he was here? At least at Ellie's he wouldn't be alone. Until he heard back from Ben Donaley, though, it was best to stay put. For now, there was no reason to alarm his wife, so he would keep the latest developments from her for now.

"Thanks for the news," he told Mara. "Give Sarah my love."

The sandwich he made from the leftover meat in the refrigerator tasted like cardboard, even though it was his favorite, roast beef. Thor scarfed it up, though, when he threw two thirds of it onto the kitchen floor for his dog.

Before leaving, Ken had slipped him a key to his gun case. He went through it, becoming familiar with the weapons inside. He loaded two pistols and strapped them to his body with cross-shoulder holsters that he found inside the gun case, and he jammed all the extra ammo he could into every available pocket on the clothes he was wearing. Lastly, he loaded the shotgun Ken carried on duty and then he sat on the living room sofa waiting, staring at a movie on the TV screen without even seeing what it was about.

When Ben Donaley called several hours later, the good news that Ellie and Anna were safe was quickly offset by the report that the SWAT team had arrived at Erin's house and had found it necessary to back off while Carlos inched his way to a waiting vehicle while hiding behind a barefoot, towel-clad Erin, and holding a gun pointed beneath her chin. Clutched in one of her arms was a pair of jeans and what looked like another piece of clothing.

"We've had to back off for now for Erin's safety," Ben Donaley told him. "We need to figure out where he's taking her." Boxing Carlos in or agitating him would surely cost Erin her life.

In anticipation of just such an escape, several patrol cars had taken up positions hidden off the road at strategic locations all the way up the mountain to Ellie's ranch. Not one of them made a move as Carlos sped by, police choosing instead to keep him under surveillance, and each time ensuring the next car up that Erin was still alive.

By the time Carlos reached the old trestle bridge on the Old Glenn Highway leading away from the Butte, he had already passed at least three squad cars hidden in this way.

By the time he reached Ellie's ranch up Knik River Road, he had passed at least five more. Earlier, in anticipation of Carlos' arrival, Ben Donaley had situated himself in the hangar in his quarters, and Doug Williams had done the same in the bunkhouse.

As everyone had suspected he would do, Carlos soon turned into Ellie's driveway, where he sat in the yard with the engine turned off for several minutes. Peeking through the curtained window of the bunkhouse, Doug could see Carlos grasping Erin's chin, and with his face very close to hers. From the hangar, Ben Donaley could hear Carlos' voice, recognizable by its thick accent.

"Get out like you're just here for a friendly little visit," Carlos hissed at Erin. "Ask the Williams woman if she's seen your mother's bankbook in the belongings of her dead old man. Pretend like you think you misplaced it when you came by to pick up your mother's things. And make it seem real, Erin, or I'm going to have to insist that you join my loving Imelda in heaven."

Doug saw Erin nod meekly before watching Carlos lean over and push the car door open and then give her a hard shove. Somewhere along the way she had gotten dressed and was wearing a man's shirt and a pair of jeans that she clumsily zipped up as she hurried toward the house.

He was tempted to blast Carlos dead right then and there, but he held himself in check as he watched Erin walk, barefoot, up to the door and knock.

CHAPTER FIFTY-EIGHT

Full Circle

DOUG WATCHED FROM INSIDE THE BUNKHOUSE AND COCKED BOTH PIS-tols as Ben made his move.

"Hi Erin, looking for Ellie?" Ben called from across the yard as he stepped out from the hangar.

"Go, Thor," Doug said, sending Thor out the bunkhouse door in a full run toward the car that held Carlos Antoya. As expected, Thor ran off into the woods the moment he saw Carlos' gun, giving Doug the time he needed to step outside with guns drawn while Carlos was distracted.

"The door's unlocked, Erin! Get inside," Ben yelled, watching as she pushed through to safety.

At that moment, Carlos jumped out of his vehicle and began spraying Ellie's front door with gunfire from an automatic weapon, forcing Doug to crouch for cover—unable to get off any shots.

When Carlos spun toward Doug, Ben Donaley fired off two shots. Scream-ing in pain, Carlos clutched one arm with the other as blood poured through his fingers and onto the gun that had fallen to the ground.

"Put the gun down, old man," someone hissed behind Ben before ordering Doug: "Drop yours, too, punk, or the old man is a goner. Ah, what the..., I'll just take care of him right now."

Before he could kill or seriously injure Ben, D.J. Carlson fell to the ground with one solid, well-placed .45 round in his back. The first officer of a swarm of police arriving on the scene stepped over D.J.'s lifeless body and fixed his gun on Carlos.

"I'll just take you and the punk kid down myself," Carlos hissed at Ben, having finally pulled another gun from his jacket pocket before he was suddenly pushed to the ground. Writhing in pain, he struggled against the force that pushed his arms high against his back with one hand, and held the cold metal of a gun to his head with the other.

Straining to free himself, Carlos grimaced and fought, but each time he moved his attacker tightened his grip.

"If you even as much as act like yer gonna flinch, it'll be the last time you ever see your self a whole man again," a voice said softly in that rhythmic monotone that Mara would have recognized had she been there.

Carlos stopped resisting, leading his captor to slightly lighten his grip. Taking advantage of the moment, he tried to jerk his arms free, but his efforts only met with them being pushed more tightly against his back.

"Wouldn't blame ya if ya finished him off, Joe," Ben Donaley said to the man who had Carlos pinned to the ground. "No one here's gonna see anything."

"I killed better than him in Nam, and there we called 'em the enemy," Joe answered.

"Tempting as it is, a quick death's too good for this piece-a…" Joe said.

When Sal pulled up in her old beater truck with Mara on the seat beside her, Joe Michael stood holding Carlos Antoya, one of the Mexican drug cartels fiercest leaders, down on the ground with all the strength he had left at the age of 66. Tired and winded, Joe got up slowly as members of the SWAT team relieved him and led Carlos Antoya away.

Joe stood there, catching his breath. If not for Mara and her long-dead father, he wouldn't even be here. Later, after he rested, he would tell Mara the whole story of how her father had pulled him back from stepping on a land mine during their combat time in the jungles of Vietnam. He would tell her how he had vowed then, to always look after the man who saved his life, and how he had promised he would watch out for his friend's only daughter when he learned that the Agent Orange sprayed on him by his own government in the fields would take him away from his daughter while she was yet a child.

He would tell her how his own personal tragedy had almost made him forget that promise to her father, until the day he found himself in line ahead of her boarding the Alaska State Ferry, and heard her give her name at the ticket counter as he stood only a few feet away. All of this, he would tell her later, after he rested—but he would find there would be no need, as Sal would have already told Mara the story.

With Carlos Antoya in custody and D.J. Carlson dead, Doug watched Mara walk up to Joe and wrap her arms around him, cradling the head of the tired old man in her bosom while she kissed him on top of his head. He watched her walk back to the truck with her arm around Joe's shoulders, where Sal pushed the truck door open and welcomed him inside.

After Mara had closed the door behind Joe, Doug watched her stand there with tears streaming down her face as Sal drove Joe away. For some reason he just stood there, leaving her standing alone, as the arrest of Carlos Antoya played out in slow motion in the background.

CHAPTER FIFTY-NINE

Headquarters— again

Ken Tandry took a statement from everyone at the scene before returning to headquarters to begin to file the charges against Carlos Antoya. Two days later, he met with Doug, Mara, Ben Donaley, and Karen Steele in his office. He had earlier met with Erin De la Corte, who had agreed to file charges against her former lover that included rape and forcible entry.

Erin had also been encouraged to, and had agreed to give a statement detailing her knowledge about the murder of Ethan Shepherd and her suspicions—based on Carlos' own statements to her—that Imelda Antoya's "tragic accident" had been no accident at all.

According to Ken Tandry, Monica De la Corte had also filed a witness statement implicating Carlos in the beating of Angus De la Corte, after overhearing Carlos acknowledge his responsibility to Erin when he did not realize that she was within earshot.

Other matters, such as the barn fire at Erin's ranch, had already been found to be arson, and police were attempting to link either Carlos or his accomplice, D.J., to that crime. Additionally, Carlos Antoya would be charged with felony stalking of Erin De la Corte.

"How about Joe Michael and Sal?" Mara asked, worried that the two had been dragged into something that neither of them deserved.

"Sal Kindle has stepped forward and given us an eyewitness statement on the murder of Santiago Antoya," Tandry said, "And Joe Micheal has committed no crime and will actually be receiving a citation from both the Palmer Police Department and the IPA recognizing his valor in bringing Carlos Antoya to justice."

"Joe did ask me to tell you," Karen Steele said, walking into the station off the street followed by Ben Donaley, "not to count on the 'lifetime' tickets for the ferry anymore."

"Oh," Mara said looking down. "I'm sorry if I used mine too often."

"It's nothing like that," Karen Steele said. "It's more a matter of there being no such thing as lifetime tickets for the ferry."

"But, then, how…" Doug interrupted.

"Apparently Joe had an arrangement with the managers of the ferry that he should be billed anytime either you or Mara showed up," Karen said. "They had his credit card on file along with his written permission to use it whenever necessary to help you both."

Mara fought back tears.

Karen Steele smoothed her skirt and opened a file folder she had been holding, consciously avoiding looking at Mara. After clearing her throat, she began:

"There is still the matter of both federal and international charges pending on both of you for unlawful flight from an agent of the IPA and for…"

"Cut the bull, daughter," Ben Donaley said, stepping forward and taking the folder from Karen Steele's hands.

"There's not a soul in this room who doesn't know you are my daughter, Brad Edwards' sister, and Mara Williams' here, sister-in-law, Beth."

Ben Donaley proceeded to take the folder from Karen Steele, tear up the papers inside, and feed them into the paper shredder next to Tandry's desk.

"None of this happened," he said, looking her straight in the eye.

"But…" Karen Steele began.

"Look Beth, you know and I know that these two were not evading anyone except the lunatic who was trying to harm them, and who is responsible for the mess that killed Brad, Dan Williams and Amanda Carlson. On top of that," he continued, "I am going to be retiring from the IPA as of—well—as of today," he said, plunking his badge down on the counter, "And, I'm going to expect you to do everything you can to wrap up this case, get Carlos Antoya convicted, and clear the name of Erin De la Corte and everyone else drawn into this sordid mess by the likes of Antoya."

Karen Steele's face flushed as she stood staring at her father in disbelief.

"And then, Beth, I am going to implore you to follow my lead and retire from this lifestyle as an international agent, settle down with that guy you're planning to marry, and give me a grandchild for young Anna to play with."

"I'm too old to play with babies, Mr. Ben," Anna said indignantly as she walked into the room with her mother.

"Don't you think you should call him by his new name of Daddy Ben?" Ellie said to her daughter, before turning to the others and announcing, "Ben and I got married at the courthouse this morning. Ken and Sarah were witnesses. My name is Ellie Edwards now—we married under Ben's real name, which is, for those of you who don't know, is Benton Edwards."

It was all too much for Mara, who sat on the sofa in Ken's office and laid her head back, closing her eyes.

"It's okay, Aunt Mara, "Anna said. "I was shocked, too—well, not really if you want the truth."

Even Mara had to laugh at the way the young girl took on such a tone of authority.

"Mommy's been lonely since Daddy went to heaven and Daddy visited me in my sleep and told me he really liked Mr. Ben and that I should just let Mr. Ben be my new daddy," Anna said.

Putting her hands on her hips again, Anna continued," I was wondering when they were going to get around to just doing it and getting married! You know?"

By now, everyone in the room was laughing and congratulating Ellie and Ben.

"I don't want to break up the festivities," Ken Tandry said, taking on a serious tone. "But in order to close all this out, I think it's important for everyone here to know—and Ben brought this to my attention this morning—that the burning of the *Fire Ring Roamer* and the surrounding incidents of vandalism of that vessel, have been determined to be the work of a faction of the Mexican cartel who were operating under the orders of Carlos Antoya."

"But why?" Doug gasped.

"Scare tactics and retaliation," Ken said simply, "for their belief that you and Mara knew more about the missing money A.C. hid than you actually did."

Doug was shaken. He had left his past and Mara's past behind him, but forces stronger than both of them had put their new life together dangerously close to being destroyed. Why? Was he cursed? Was she?

"Son," Ben Donaley said, putting his arm on Doug's shoulder. "It's over now. You and Mara are alive and neither Carlos Antoya nor his henchmen are going to bother you again."

"But how can we be sure?" Doug said, rising from his chair. "We thought we were okay before."

"Because the South American cartel knows we have Carlos Antoya in custody, and they know that D.J. is dead," Ben Donaley said. "Apparently, before he was shot, D.J. told his contacts there that he had found the money owed them under the barn on Sassy's property, and sent them the full amount in an effort to save his own hide and keep them from discovering that, like his father, he was a double agent. As far as they are concerned, it was Carlos Antoya who swindled them. They have no further interest in anything that transpired with D.J. Carlson simply by the fact that, in their eyes, he swindled their archrival, Carlos Antoya, to their benefit, got him locked up in the process, and is now himself dead. Any other money that might turn up belongs to Carlos Antoya and Carlos Antoya will never try to claim it, as doing so would only serve to cement his guilt. With all the evidence we have, Carlos Antoya will spend..."

Doug's eyes were wide with disbelief as Ben's voice faded into just so much blah, blah, blah in the background.

"It's over, Doug," Ben Donaley said gently, bringing Doug back into focus. "All of it is over. Except for the loss of your boat, you can go back to living your life without fear."

CHAPTER SIXTY

New Beginning

On June 1, only weeks after the incident that had brought Carlos Antoya to justice, Doug, Mara, Sarah, Ken, and their new baby boy they called "B.D."—named after Brad Edwards and Dan Williams—gathered in the yard at Erin De la Corte's home in the Butte for the official kickoff to the memorial that Erin was having built as a tribute to her birth mother, Sassy. Even Sassy's—and now Erin's—caretaker, Stan, shed a tear as the excavators pulled the first shovelful of dirt out of the ground.

On this day which would have been Amanda Carlson's 38th birthday, Erin stood before the growing crowd to unveil the plans for constructing a large, raised, circular green area in the middle of the ranchland that had been so central to the happiest moments of her mother's life. In the distance, Pioneer Peak, still covered in snow, stood in all its jagged splendor against the other equally spectacular mountains that ringed the Mat-Su Valley.

As little B.D. cried out in his mother's arms, Erin asked those attending for one last moment of their attention.

"I also want to announce to all of you that just as my mother was when she bore me, I am pregnant under the terrible circumstances of which you are all aware. Like my mother, who chose to let me come into this world, I am planning to carry my baby—a girl—to term. Unlike my mother, though, who was unable to keep me, it is my intention to keep my baby.

I wish my birth mother could have been here to meet little Amanda Monica De la Corte when she arrives at the beginning of next year, but I also know that her grandparents, Monica and Angus, will join me in giving her all the love she needs to one day grow up to manage this very ranch."

As the crowd broke out in spontaneous applause, Erin stepped down from the podium she had been standing on and ushered those attending past the architect's rendition of what the completed project would look like.

There would be an oval track for exercising the horses—much like the design of a small racetrack. Within the fenced oval would be the green space—raised and consisting of a wide array of trees like the weeping birch and spruce that her mother had loved so much, and apple trees for the horses to nibble on. There would be plenty of chunks of natural granite rocks, as well as areas of indigenous perennials—like lupine, fireweed and cotton grass—and raised rock beds for annuals to be planted. When finished, the area would resemble a natural landscape and would be a place of beauty all year round. A simple plaque would read, *Dedicated to the memory of Amanda "Sassy" Carlson.*

The track itself would be heated, so that the horses could run on it year round. The stables would be expanded to accommodate more horses, and Stan would be promoted to head stable master in charge of running the place, leaving Erin free to travel between Palmer and Santa Barbara.

"Thanks to a generous donation by Angus and Monica De la Corte," Erin told the crowd, "my birth mother will be remembered for the good she brought to this earth."

The excavator creaked and groaned as it lifted two more shovelfuls of dirt, before a loud clank caused its operator to downshift the motor and jump down on the vehicle's track to see what obstacle lay beneath the ground.

"Looks like an old buried tank or something," he said. "I'll get some more equipment in here to pull it up tomorrow."

After a reception inside the stables, those who had attended slowly dispersed—including the members of the entire Palmer Police Department and other law enforcement officials who had been instrumental in the capture of Carlos Antoya.

"I mean no disrespect to your own cousin," Ken Tandry told Erin, "but like his father, A.C., D.J. was a bad seed. I'm sorry it cost your mother her life to learn that very unfortunate lesson."

"You owe me no apology," Erin told Tandry. "I never even knew of his existence."

When Sarah joined the two, she handed B.D. to Erin and asked her to hold him for a minute while she got something out of her purse.

"He's beautiful," Erin said simply.

"I just wanted you to hold him so you will know what you have to look forward to with your own baby," Sarah said.

"Your mother would have been so proud of you," Doug added, as he and Mara stopped to say goodbye on their way out. "It looks like time for a new beginning here at Sassy's old place. It's a wonderful end to what ended up being a very sad story. I hope you won't mind if I stay in touch and drop by from time to time."

"You're always welcome here," Erin said, wrapping her arms around Doug and kissing him on the cheek. "Always."

"Oh, of course I meant you, too," she said to Mara, as if suddenly realizing she was standing there. "Both of you are always welcome here."

CHAPTER SIXTY-ONE

Unexpected "Cache"

MARA WAS ROCKING B.D. AND DOUG WAS WORKING OUT IN THE YARD WITH Ken when the call came in summoning Ken to Erin De la Corte's ranch.

"I couldn't believe it, myself, when I saw it," Wes, the excavator, said, as he and Ken Tandry stared at the huge safe that had just been pulled from the ground.

"Better get Karen Steele down here—and Ben Donaley, too," Tandry said. "Retired or not, Ben's gonna want to see this."

Once Ben and Karen had arrived, a decision was made to call in a locksmith to open the safe. A short time later, in spite of severe rust, the locksmith was able to get it open before leaving without waiting to see what was inside.

"Just invoice the Palmer Police Department, Bill," Tandry called after the man he had known for more than thirty years.

"Will do," Bill nodded, as he climbed into his truck and drove off.

Erin stood with the others staring at the huge, black box. The day was sunny and warm by Alaska standards, but she had not yet adjusted to the subarctic climate and wore a down jacket to insulate her from the cold breeze coming from the direction of the two massive glaciers to the east of the valley that held her ranch. Looking down at the safe, she was the first to see the engraving in the center of the dull, black metal of the safe's door: *Property of Adam "A.C." Carlson.*

"Any idea of when he might have had this buried?" Ken Tandry asked Stan, who had walked out from the barn to join the others.

"I couldn't say for absolute sure," Stan said, "But about two years ago, Sassy had A.C. move into her place so's she could keep an eye on him."

"I remember that," Doug, who had arrived with Mara, Sarah and the baby, said. "I remember it because Sassy and I were dating pretty steadily then…" Doug paused and looked at his wife, embarrassed.

"Go ahead, Doug," Mara said. "It's no secret you and Sassy were a couple long before we ever met."

Looking a bit relieved, Doug continued, "I remember Sassy telling me that A.C. was going to do some work in the pasture area. She and I were pretty much staying up at Dan and Ellie's then, and I remember her running back to her place one time and coming back fuming that A.C. had torn up all the pasture and hadn't even reseeded it. Eventually, she took care of that herself, with the help of Stan."

"That's right," Stan said. "And that woulda been right about the time I had to fly back East for my sister's funeral. I remember Miss Carlson bein' madder'n blazes about the way A.C. left the pasture and then moved back into town leavin' her to tidy everything up."

"I'm guessin' we're gonna find a nice stash of both cash and guns inside that safe," Ben Donaley said, after stepping out of the truck he had pulled up in moments earlier.

Suddenly, Thor was running toward the truck, jumping inside to lick both Ellie and Anna before Mara could stop him.

"Doug, Thor!" she said to her husband.

Doug hollered for Thor to come back and Thor looked at him momentarily before ignoring him to play with Anna, who had just jumped down out of the truck.

"I'm sorry, Ellie," Mara said, walking up to her friend. "I hope Thor didn't make a mess."

"Mara, you worry too much. We all love Thor," Ellie answered, quickly changing the subject. "What's going on here?"

"The excavator just dug up this safe and it says it's the property of A.C." Mara answered. "I think they're about ready to open it."

As everyone watched, Ken Tandry and two officers tried to pull the door to the safe open. When that didn't work, they enlisted the help of Wes, who backed up to it with a loader and hooked a chain through a hole that once held the lock. He then inched the loader forward until the door came loose.

Inside were dozens of boxes that Ben Donaley described as old military issue ammo cases. They counted fifty boxes in all. Opening the first one, he pulled out 10 bundles of one hundred-dollar-bills, each bundle holding ten bills. Upon further examination, each of the fifty boxes was found to contain the exact same amount of cash.

"Looks like A.C. was organized. There's half a million dollars right here," Ben Donaley said.

In addition to the ammo cases, there were ten sealed metal cases that each held five high-powered rifles. In several other boxes found inside the safe, were enough rounds of ammunition to support nothing short of full-blown warfare. Markings on both the guns and the ammo showed that they were manufactured in Russia—somehow smuggled into Alaska, according to Ben Donaley. Immediately, he ordered the weapons and ammunition confiscated by law enforcement, who would move them to a secure location where they would later be destroyed.

Lastly, inside the safe, was a small box containing a passport showing A.C.'s picture but listing his name as Adolfo Carlton, as well as another wad of bills totaling two hundred fifty thousand dollars, a photo of A.C. as a child standing next to his sister, Amanda, and an old rosary with a crucifix upon which the initials *r.i.p. A.C.* were scratched on the back.

"If I'm not mistaken, and Ken Tandry can officially verify this," Ben Donaley said, "It looks like Erin De la Corte, who if as we suspect is the last living relative of Adam Carlson, is now three quarters of a million dollars richer."

Erin gasped and clutched Karen Steele's arm, while Doug and Mara just stared at each other, looking as dumbfounded as everyone else.

CHAPTER SIXTY-TWO

Real No More

"NOTHING SEEMS REAL ANYMORE," DOUG SAID TO MARA LATER, AS THEY walked back to their truck.

"Don't get me wrong, I'm happy that Erin made out so well—sure as heck better than I did," he said with a hollow laugh.

Mara stood beside the man she had married less than a year ago and, for the first time, saw a shell of the self-sufficient, pillar of strength that she had first been drawn to. She had changed, too, but Doug was crumbling. Whereas she had grown stronger and more self-sufficient, he had suddenly lost his spark and seemed to be floundering. She put her hand on his arm, but he pulled away, giving her the answer to the question she hadn't even yet had time to think of.

"I don't know what I'm going to do now," he said, mostly to himself.

His voice was eerily bland, not the booming voice of the self-assured guy she had married.

"No boat, no real job skills to speak of . . ." he mumbled, letting his voice trail off.

Doug watched Ken and Sarah walk to their car with B.D.. They had nothing but years of happiness ahead of them now that Ken was going to retire and pursue his dream of starting his own business. The pangs of jealousy that surfaced made him look away.

Off in the distance, Thor was playing with young Anna, while Ben Donaley and his new bride, Ellie, held hands. Dan would be happy to know that Ellie had found happiness again, and that Anna would have such a wonderful new father as Benton Edwards surely would be—at least someone was lucky enough to be living his brother's life now.

For some reason Erin's face popped into his consciousness. She, too, had found new purpose in rebuilding her mother's legacy and in soon becoming a mother herself. Even the mysterious Joe Michael had found love with Sal Kindle, and could now put his own heartache behind him. Everywhere Doug looked, the people in his life had moved past the horrors of the past two years. Why couldn't he?

There were a couple of worthy seiners for sale down in Homer and another in Dutch Harbor. Maybe he'd fly down and check them out, or maybe he'd take a year off and just do nothing. Maybe he would do neither. Maybe he'd look for another job, or maybe he'd just not think about it right now.

When Mara walked away to talk to Sarah, he barely took notice, nor did he when she walked back. When he heard her call them goodbye, her words intruded on his senses—an unwelcome interruption in the mind-set that was beginning to engulf every fiber of who he had ever been.

"Doug? Do you think we should head for home?" Mara said.

Almost reflexly, the words spilled out.

"Home? We don't have a home, Mara—do we? I mean, we have your house in Homer, but…"

"Our house," she interrupted. Why was Doug behaving this way?

"You bought that house for yourself when you moved to Alaska to start your new life after Brad died. It's your house, Mara. It's supposed to be your house."

"It's our house, Doug," she said, as she brushed newly formed tears away with the back of her hand.

"Did I say something…do something…," she began, but Doug stopped her and took her hands into his own.

"This is not going to be easy, Mara," he began, "either for me, or for you. As a matter of fact, until this very moment, I didn't even know I felt this way."

Mara pulled her hand away from his. As quickly as the tears had begun, they stopped. He couldn't be going here. No way.

"I meant it when I said I loved you," Doug told her, "And I entered into our marriage with all the hope and passion I had ever dreamed of holding."

Now Doug had tears in his eyes.

"There's no good way to say this," he continued. "I need to be alone now."

"Okay," Mara said, "I can go down to Homer for a few days until you sort out your thoughts…"

"No, Mara," he said, "I mean alone, as in…alone…permanently…at least for the foreseeable future. It's not you, it's me…"

Doug's words were lost to her ears from there. She had heard of this old break up cliché a million times, never thinking the words would be said to her—especially not now, and by the man she loved. Stunned, she tried to maintain her composure, but her mind was racing. Why? Why? She struggled for the answer. She had already lost so much with the Brad. Why this? Why now?

"Don't say anymore, Doug," she said with steely calm, summoning up all her newfound strength. "Just don't say one single solitary word more."

"But Mara…it's not you…"

"I said, don't—say—one—word—more," she repeated, slowly emphasizing each of the words with a shuddering reserve that made him step back.

She slid the solid gold band he had given her on their wedding day off her ring finger, pressed it gently into his palm, closed his fingers around it, and walked slowly away. There was no reason to belabor the point, to give it one more moment of energy, or to fight for what obviously was not even there. Her new reality was that there had been no old reality. From the first moment she had arrived in Alaska, and even before, nothing that had happened had turned out to be what it appeared.

She had suffered the greatest loss she could ever imagine and then suffered it a second time when Brad had seemingly come back from the dead before being brutally taken from her again. Yet, had he ever really been hers in the first place? She had suffered learning of his lies and struggled to know what were truths. She had no more energy to put into reliving a similar scenario again with a different man.

From her pocket she withdrew two scraps of paper and saw that they were the ferry tickets given to her in Homer by Joe Michael. She let them fall to the ground, unmindful of the rain that was beginning to fall. She stood there in the rain, watching the ink smudge and become illegible—not that it mattered, anyway. Like her marriage to Doug, they, too, apparently weren't real.

Thor ran to her and she held him, emptying her tears into the fur on his neck. She held tightly to him and he stood firm, letting her. Her tears turned to sobs and her sobs to heaving gasps, but through it all, Thor held her up. When there were no more tears to fall, Thor licked her face. He licked her nose and then her eyes and licked her fingers. For a moment, he looked into her swollen eyes with his own hauntingly gold ones and told her that he loved her with the language that dogs use to communicate with humans. When he knew she would be okay, he walked slowly back to the man who had raised him from a pup and watched her walk away.

Later, toward fall, silhouetted against a heavy mist, a lone figure stood for the second time in their lives on an unnamed beach in Hoonah, facing a totem that had a red dot at the top of a feather carved on the long side and facing upward. When the fog lifted minutes later, both the figure and the dot were gone, leaving one to wonder in the sound of the gentle lap of the waves if more than the present stillness had ever really been there.

www.ingramcontent.com/pod-product-compliance
Lightning Source LLC
Chambersburg PA
CBHW051957090426
42741CB00008B/1436